SLS Monograph Series

New subscribers to *Sign Language Studies* quickly discover the gems contained in back issues of the joural. Because many of the back issues of this quarterly journal are no longer available in print, readers have often requested that those gems be made available in a more convienient format. *SLS Monographs* is offered as a direct response to those requests. Each monograph will be devoted to a single topic and will select from pertinent articles that have appeared in *Sign Language Studies*. In some cases the articles will serve to trace the development of a particular line of theoretical inquiry and research. In other cases the articles represent descriptive and empirical research on a given topic. *SLS Monographs* will be useful as texts in Interpreter Education Programs, Sign Language classes, and Deaf Studies programs.

A portion of the proceeds from sales of *SLS Monographs* will be donated to the Stokoe Scholarship Fund. This scholarship is administered by the National Association of the Deaf. Scholarships are awarded annually to deaf graduate students to support their studies of Sign Language and/or the deaf community. Donations from proceeds will be made annually in the name of the authors whose work appears in this *SLS Monograph*.

For more information about the Stokoe Scholarship please contact the NAD. For more information about *Sign Language Studies*, the *SLS Monograph* series, and other scholarly publications on Sign Language and the deaf community contact:

Linstok Press
4020 Blackburn Lane
Burtonsville, MD 20866

Published by
Linstok Press
4020 Blackburn Lane
Burtonsville, MD 20866

ISBN 0-932130-11-9

Contents

2

Preface

The chapters that follow first appeared in a special issue of the journal *Sign Language Studies*, volume 59, published in the summer of 1988. For this monograph we have added an additional chapter by Tom Humphries, entitled "An Introduction to the Culture of Deaf People in the U.S.: Content Notes and Reference Material for Teachers." This article first appeared in *Sign Language Studies*, 72, 209–240, 1991.

Humphries' chapter is the perfect addition to those which are reprinted here. As I noted in 1988, one of the strongest objections to the notion that ASL can and should meet foreign language requirements is often made by those who claim that users of ASL have distinct culture. Humphries' chapter not only adds to the evidence that such a culture does indeed exist, but demonstrates how cultural information about Deaf people can effectively be taught to students of ASL.

I would like to thank the many people who have helped to make the special issue of *Sign Language Studies* and this volume become a reality: Nancy Frishberg and Susan Rutherford for their encouragement and direction; William Stokoe for making available the expanded edition of *Sign Language Studies*; Dennis Cokely for his enthusiasm in including this volume in the Sign Media/Linstok Press *SLS Monographs* series; and, of course, the authors.

Sherman Wilcox
February 1992
Albuquerque, NM

Introduction: Academic Acceptance of American Sign Language

Sherman Wilcox
University of New Mexico

"The movement to accept ASL throughout America is like a slow-building ground swell of water," according to Gary W. Olsen, Executive Director of the National Association of the Deaf. "It gains momentum as it swells and so is the acceptance of ASL." Undoubtedly true, but the ground swell has been slow to emerge in academia. Although ASL has a long and rich history in America and scholarly research on ASL is in its third decade, ASL has been slow to garner any degree of status in the academic community. As recently as 1980, for example, Battison and Carter (1981:viii) conceded that "as far as we know, no colleges or university has yet made Sign Language a permanent part of its foreign language curricula, on a par with the other foreign languages they teach."

This situation is beginning to change (Wilcox & Wilcox, 1991). The issue of academic acceptance of ASL "has come up, and by all indications is going to keep coming up" (Chapin, this volume). Consider my own experience. In the period from August 1987 to April 1988, I was contacted by individuals in California, New York, Ohio, Illinois, Missouri, Wyoming, Massachusetts, Iowa, and several other states; by representatives of Boards of Regents for university systems in Tennessee and Massachusetts; by state commissions for the deaf, colleges and universities, state departments of education, state legislatures, and the news media. The other authors in this special issue could relate the same story.

One possible explanation for this recent surge of interest in acceptance of ASL as a foreign language may be the fact that many educational institutions which had dropped foreign language requirements are now reinstituting them. Our current round of educational reforms, however, often has been driven by economic motivations. When applied to the question of foreign language instruction these motivations are sometimes used to argue against acceptance of ASL. The essence of the claim is that traditional foreign languages such as French or German must be taught because professionals need to read scholarly literature in them; there is a vocational motivation for learning one of these languages that does not exist for ASL.

Even if we could justify vocationalism as the only or most important goal of education, and I believe we cannot (see, for example, Dewey 1916), the appeal to vocational criteria to justify foreign language requirements does not hold. In an address to a joint meeting of the Washington and Oregon Association of Foreign Language Teachers, Glenn Crosby, a professor of chemistry and chemical physics, asked whether scientists need foreign languages to practice their craft. His answer was that they do not. Still, Dr. Crosby supported foreign language requirements for undergraduate students. "Foreign language acquisition is necessary," he maintained, "to be an educated, sentient person with empathy for foreign peoples and cultures and a capacity to experience the world through other eyes, other words, and from other orientations. Explain to undergraduates or high school students that their lives will be immeasurably impoverished without an understanding of the relationship of language to culture and of language to thought" (Crosby, 1987:183). These reasons are entirely compatible with the arguments put forward here in support of ASL as a foreign language.

Paul Chapin opens this special issue by examining the educational purposes of foreign language requirements. One of the goals of studying a foreign language, he asserts, is to understand language as a structured system. Even a brief exposure to a different language compels students to confront language at a more abstract level. Students come away from this experience with a fuller appreciation of their own language and with a sense of the awesome, but still poorly understood, human language ability.

"ASL serves this purpose admirably" (Chapin, this volume). Victoria Fromkin, the distinguished linguist and Dean of the Graduate School at UCLA, provides a concise tutorial on the linguistics of ASL in which she points out that the scientific study of this language establishes beyond a doubt that it *is* a natural language distinct from English. Fromkin shows that by examining ASL we can gain insight into how the abstract cognitive system we call language finds expression in the signed modality. Moreover, if language is a 'mirror of the mind', then research which compares and contrasts signed and spoken languages provides us with the parallax needed to glean a sharper view of the human language ability.

"Another purpose of second language study is to give the student entree into another culture" (Chapin, this volume). Susan Rutherford provides an overview of the other culture that ASL students learn about and enter, Deaf culture. She takes on some of the most difficult questions lodged against acceptance of ASL as a foreign language — Is there a culture or are deaf people merely a heterogeneous group of handicapped Americans? Isn't Deaf culture merely a subculture? — and provides solid answers well-rooted in the anthropological study of culture.

Foreign language study should also "expose the student to a new, different mode of aesthetic expression" (Chapin, this volume). The perceived lack of literature in ASL is serious and one of the most difficult charges to answer in gaining acceptance of ASL as a foreign language. Nancy Frishberg's article on the literary status of ASL breaks new, exciting ground. She points out that ASL, although currently lacking an accepted writing system, nevertheless supports a rich literary tradition. Her article is one of the first to discuss oral and written traditions in relation to ASL, ASL being understood as an "oral" language. Frishberg's argument is significant not only because it broadens our understanding of ASL literature, but also because it will encourage exploration of related issues such as the influence of oral strategies in deaf children's signing and writing (Wilcox 1982).

Merely advocating for acceptance of ASL in fulfillment of foreign language requirements does not guarantee that ASL, as opposed to some signed version of

English, will be taught or that it will be taught correctly. Teaching ASL as a second language in the classroom setting is a relatively new field. Cheri Smith provides us with a glimpse into the planning, research, and hard work that goes into the development of an ASL curriculum. Readers with experience in language teaching will immediately notice that the process that Smith describes is the same one that a teacher of French, German, or Spanish would use to develop a course curriculum.

Knowing what to teach is not enough. Language teachers must have certain qualifications and skills, and teachers of ASL are no exception. As Kanda and Fleischer note, "it is no longer enough just to 'sign well' or to 'be deaf'." In their discussion of who is qualified to teach ASL, they recognize that language teachers must know and respect the language, must know the principles of second language instruction, and must be good teachers. The standards they propose for ASL teachers are reasonable and greatly needed. It is one thing to propose high standards; it is quite another, though, to convince people already in the field to listen to you and to accede to the painful process of upgrading their skills. By recognizing that language teachers are first and foremost human beings, Kanda and Fleischer ground their call for high standards in a humanistic respect for the thousands of ASL teachers already in the field who bring out the best in their students and themselves.

Stephen Wilbers places the study of ASL and Deaf culture squarely in the mainstream of American liberal education. Reading his article, I was reminded of the

words of the Mexican poet, Octavio Paz (1967), who
wrote:

> What sets worlds in motion is the interplay of
> differences, their attractions and repulsions. Life
> is plurality.... By suppressing differences and pe-
> culiarities, by eliminating different civilizations
> and cultures, progress weakens life... Every view
> of the world that becomes extinct, every culture
> that disappears, diminishes a possibility of life.

Wilbers pleads instead for a progress that accepts
differences, that encourages pluralism, and that em-
braces different cultures within our society — a
progress that acknowledges and respects Black, Asian,
Indian, Hispanic, Deaf, and all the various other possibilities of life.

Academic acceptance of ASL is not limited to the
college level. Peggy Selover's excellent work in support of legislation to accept ASL as a foreign language
credit in California's high schools establishes an example which the rest of the country will certainly follow.
In her article, she explains how this legislation was
adopted and raises issues regarding the implementation of the law which many readers will want to consider.

Selover clearly reveals that successful efforts to
gain acceptance of ASL involve considerable hard
work. The process is often long and arduous. A history
of the process to accept ASL in fulfillment of the foreign language requirement at the University of New
Mexico is chronicled in Lamb and Wilcox's article. As
they demonstrate, success sometimes depends not so
much on presenting the right facts as in the process of
discovering and sharing those facts.

In the final analysis, it seems to me that there are two compelling reasons to advocate for academic acceptance of ASL. One is what the language has to offer. Languages are tools, not only for communicating ideas but for exploring ideas. ASL is, in my opinion, a wonderful pedagogical tool for sharpening the intellect, exploring the world, and testing research hypotheses.

The second reason concerns what academia has to offer the language, its culture, and its speakers. We must not lose sight of the fact that ASL is a minority, suppressed language, and that its speakers and their culture historically have been oppressed and poorly understood. The recent appointment of a hearing candidate with no background in ASL or Deaf culture to become president of Gallaudet University, the subsequent galvanizing of the nation's deaf communities, and eventual selection of Gallaudet's *first* deaf president, are eloquent testimony to this.

Harlan Lane has written passionately and cogently about the oppression of ASL and its speakers (Lane 1984). Here, he offers suggestions for incorporating ASL and Deaf culture into a bilingual/bicultural approach to deaf education. His recommendations provide a glimpse of how a better understanding of ASL and Deaf culture could have radical implications for deaf education in America.

Finally, David Armstrong of Gallaudet University addresses the implications of widespread acceptance of ASL by hearing people. He echoes the warning issued by Gary W. Olsen that the ground swell of interest in ASL "can be devastating if proper precautions are not taken." One of the precautions that Armstrong recommends is that institutions of higher education should make affirmative action training and employment commitments to deaf individuals. In this way, deaf people will become full-fledged members of the academic community, and academic acceptance of ASL and its speakers will move one step closer to becoming a reality.

The facts and arguments presented by the authors in this issue are clear. The study of ASL affords the same educational values and the same intellectual rewards as the study of any other foreign language. American Sign Language has much to offer our nation's educational institutions, and they in turn have much to offer this language and its speakers. The time has come for ASL to take its rightful place in American education.

References

Battison, R. and S. M. Carter. 1981. "The academic status of sign language." In F. Caccamise, M. Garretson, and U. Bellugi (eds.), *Teaching American Sign Language as a second/foreign language.* Proceedings of the Third National Symposium on Sign Language Research and Teaching. Silver Spring, MD: National Association of the Deaf.

Crosby, G. A. 1987. "Does a scientist need foreign languages?" *Foreign Language Annals,* 20, 181–183.

Dewey, J. 1916. *Democracy and Education.* NY: Macmillan.

Lane, H. 1984. *When the Mind Hears.* NY: Random House.

Paz, O. 1967. *The Labyrinth of Solitude*. London: Allen Lane, Penguin Press.

Wilcox, S. 1982. "Oral/literate strategies in deaf children's signed and written language." Paper presented at the Third Annual Ethnography in Education Research Forum, University of Pennsylvania, March 18–21.

Wilcox, S. and P. Wilcox. 1991. *Learning to See: American Sign Language as a Second Language*. Englewood Cliffs, NJ: Prentice Hall Regents (a publication of Center for Applied Linguistics).

American Sign Language and the Liberal Education

Paul G. Chapin
National Science Foundation[1]

Curricular reforms abound. Following the dire reports of some prestigious national commissions, leaders of American education at all levels are hard at work on improving their product. Math, science, and foreign language education are especially under scrutiny. Many institutions which dropped requirements in an earlier wave of reforms two decades ago are now reimposing them, or imposing new ones, foreign language requirements in particular. The time is opportune for creative thinking about the goals of education, and for applying new understanding in designing a plan for meeting those goals.

This volume, and these remarks introducing it, are devoted to the educational implications of a subject on which our understanding has advanced notably in the past two decades, American Sign Language (ASL). An issue has come up, and by all indications is going to keep coming up: should ASL instruction satisfy foreign language requirements? I suspect that to most of the

[1] The views expressed here are the author's own, and should in no way be taken as official positions of the National Science Foundation or any of its programs, or of the United States Government.

1

regular readers of this journal, the answer is obviously affirmative. Unfortunately, however, there is evidence of a certain degree of resistance to this conclusion among some of the planners and deciders of academe.

A recent case in point: A student at Pomona College in California, Paul Macdonald, petitioned his college's Academic Procedures Committee to have ASL meet his undergraduate foreign language requirement. His petition was granted, but with the clear and explicit understanding that his case was exceptional and set no precedent. Mr. Macdonald had worked extensively with the deaf community, had taken summer courses in ASL, and had spent a year at Gallaudet University. In the Committee's view these factors justified making the exception in his case, but the Committee expressed significant reservations about any change in the general policy precluding acceptance of ASL to satisfy the foreign language requirement. An article in the student newspaper, reporting the decision, quoted the Registrar as saying, "We allowed an exception to the policy.... The College is not taking a position on American Sign Language as meeting the foreign language requirement, but his request was approved." A student member of the Committee said, "There was a lot of debate on whether there is a deaf culture or whether it is just a subculture within a larger culture." Macdonald cited the concerns of the Modern Language Department, including "the lack of literature in the deaf culture, the possible lack of a 'deaf culture', and the lack of a cross-national boundary."

An earlier case in point: in 1984 the California State Universities and Colleges system began to consider the institution of a system-wide foreign language require-

ment. A Task Force was formed to study the implications. The Task Force report defined foreign language
to include "classical languages but not computer languages, artificial languages, sign languages, or dialects
of English."

Reports like these have angered many of those who
work with ASL and the deaf community; they have
seen in them indifference or outright hostility to the
language and culture of deaf people in America. I believe, however, there is a more benign interpretation.
Those who have responsibility for making the strategic
decisions about the structure and direction of education in America have well-developed ideals about
what education ought to accomplish. They have simply not yet been persuaded that ASL, taught as a foreign or second language, fits into those ideals, because
they have not yet acquired a valid understanding of
the nature of ASL, and of the people whose native language it is. Given the relative recency of reliable
knowledge among linguists and other specialists in the
area, it is not too surprising that this information has
not yet permeated the general culture. The papers in
this issue, it may be hoped, should help to fill the gap.

A fruitful way to approach the issue is to consider
just what are the educational purposes of a foreign language requirement. I see three major purposes.

The purpose which is of first importance to me as a
linguist is learning to understand language as a structured system. Years of instruction in English grammar
may never bring this point home to a student nearly so
quickly as intensive exposure for a year or two to an alternative system, one which allows you to put the same
semantic messages into very differently shaped pack-

ages, not just with different words but with different grammatical organization. ASL serves this purpose admirably, at least as well as the French or Spanish which the student would be likely to take to meet the requirement. Since systematic research revealed (by the early 1970s) that ASL is indeed a full-fledged natural language, there has been a great deal of interest and effort invested in understanding and describing its linguistic structure. We now know, for example, that ASL has verb-final word order, like Japanese or Turkish, and unlike English, French, and Spanish, which have Subject-Verb-Object word order. ASL has a much more elaborate morphology than most European languages, particularly in the expression of verbal aspect. Studying ASL will certainly compel students to confront the diversity, and the regularity, of linguistic structure, and to come to a fuller appreciation of the structure of their own native language as a result.

Another purpose of second language study is to give the student entree into another culture, and thus to broaden his or her perspective. The deaf community in the United States is clearly a subculture, pretty much by definition, but it is one which has been shown to have its own quite distinctive cultural characteristics. Susan Rutherford's paper in this issue provides a detailed examination of Deaf culture. A firsthand acquaintance with that culture can be of just as great educational value to a student as the exposure to cultural variation which accompanies any normal foreign language course. Furthermore, the study of American Deaf culture offers the language student two special educational advantages which offset any presumed disadvantages of studying a subculture. First is its immediacy. Unlike the great national cultures which the foreign language student usually confront, American Deaf culture is among us, though typically invisible to hearing persons. Indeed, the very invisibility is itself a strong argument for education and enlightenment of members of the majority culture. The second advantage is that an understanding of the deaf community depends even more crucially on some command of the community's language, ASL, than is true for other cultures one would be likely to study.

A third purpose is to expose the student to a new, different mode of aesthetic expression. ASL is a particularly apt subject of study in this respect at present. Poetry and drama in ASL are blossoming, lively fields of activity and creativity just now. The National Theater of the Deaf is winning national acclaim for its sensitive and engrossing performances, and a number of ASL poets are producing fresh and witty and sophisticated work. ASL allows the creative poet a whole new dimension of expression. Students with access to this genre are likely to find it more exciting than the classics of poetry commonly taught in other language courses.

It should be clear that the study of ASL meets the goals of second language study in ways in which the other "languages" excluded in the Task Force report mentioned earlier do not. Computer languages and artificial languages are not really languages at all, that is, not natural languages, and offer none of the educational advantages of second language study. Dialects of English are not second languages, and do not significantly diversify the student's linguistic experience. Not even all sign languages are appropriate subjects of second language study. Signed English, for example, which is sometimes used in interpretation and in educational settings for deaf students, is not a second language, but rather a coded form of ordinary English. But ASL, American Sign Language, is entirely worthy of inclusion in the curriculum of a liberal education, and the time has come for the makers of educational policy to recognize that truth.

Sign Languages: Evidence for Language Universals and the Linguistic Capacity of the Human Brain

Victoria A. Fromkin
University of California Los Angeles

> It is not the want of organs that [prevents animals from making]...known their thoughts...for it is evident that magpies and parrots are able to utter words just like ourselves, and yet they cannot speak as we do, that is, so as to give evidence that they think of what they say. On the other hand, men who, being born deaf and mute...are destitute of the organs which serve the others for talking, are in the habit of themselves inventing certain signs by which they make themselves understood.
>
> Rene Descartes *Discourse on Method*

For thousands of years, philosophers and scientists have attempted to understand the nature of human language, motivated by the historic assumption that language is a 'mirror of the mind' or that "Speech is the only window through which the physiologist can view the cerebral life," as was suggested by Fournier in 1887.

The quotation from Fournier refers to speech since there has been a persistent, though incorrect, view which equates speech with language. Speech (production and perception) is behavior, the use or performance of those who know a *spoken* language. Language is the abstract mental cognitive system which permits one to speak and understand. Language also underlies the ability of a deaf person to 'sign' and to visually perceive and understand the gestures of a signing person.

To equate speech with language is to obscure what is the nature of the linguistic systems which form the bases for all spoken languages and for all the signed languages used by communities of deaf persons throughout the world. As long as researchers concerned themselves only with spoken languages there was no way to separate what is essential to the linguistic cognitive system from the constraints imposed, productively and perceptually, by the auditory-vocal modality, that is, to discover what is the genetically, biologically determined linguistic ability of the human brain. The human brain seems to be uniquely suited for the acquisition and use of language. As noted by Geschwind (1979):

> The nervous systems of all animals have a number of basic functions in common, most notably the control of movement and the analysis of sensation. What distinguishes the human brain is the variety of more specialized activities it is capable of learning. *The preeminent example is language* (my emphasis).

Note that Geschwind speaks of language, not speech. We now know, through the work of linguists conducting research on these signed languages, first initiated by Stokoe's seminal work in 1960, that their basic similarities to spoken languages are greater than their differences, that they are subject to the same constraints on their structures, and relate forms and meanings by means of the same kinds of rules. This therefore suggests that the human brain is organically equipped for language in any modality, and that the kinds of languages which can be acquired are not determined by the motor or perceptual systems but by higher order brain mechanisms.

If this is so, then one can seek and find language universals which pertain to all human languages, a view accepted by Roger Bacon in the 13th century when he wrote

He that understands grammar in one language, understands it in another as far as the essential properties of Grammar are concerned. The fact that he can't speak, nor comprehend, another language is due to...the accidental properties of grammar.

While these accidental properties may prevent a speaker of English from understanding a speaker of Arabic, or a user of American Sign Language (ASL) from understanding a signer of Chinese Sign Language, Bacon was correct in that the more we look at all human languages the more they appear to be governed by the same universal principles and constraints, thereby supporting the view that the human brain seems to be uniquely suited for the acquisition and use of any language the child is exposed to. Both sighted hearing and deaf children can learn sign language; the reason deaf children cannot learn spoken languages with ease is because the child receives no auditory input. It is not the language ability which is lacking since deaf children have intact brains. It is therefore not surprising that deaf signers with damage to the left hemisphere show aphasia for signed language similar to the language breakdown in hearing aphasics (Poizner *et al.* 1987). What is equally interesting is that the language impairments of these patients contrast markedly with their relatively intact capacities to process non-language visual spatial relationships, further enforcing the fact that the left hemisphere has an innate predisposition for language (not speech or the physical ways in which language is expressed).

There is overwhelming evidence that reveals the essential similarities between signed languages and spoken languages supporting Bacon's insight into the nature of human language. ASL and all signed languages used in deaf communities throughout the world are subject to the same kinds of structural constraints, relate forms and meanings by means of the same kinds of recursive rules, and contain equivalent kinds of sublexical units as spoken language.

Sign languages are fully developed languages, and those who know sign language are capable of creating and comprehending unlimited numbers of new sentences just as speakers of spoken languages. Thus, neither language acquisition nor use is dependent on the ability to produce and hear sounds, but rather on a more abstract, biologically determined, cognitive ability. It is this genetically pre-wired language faculty which accounts for the similarities between spoken and signed languages.

The basic similarities between these two classes of human languages can be exemplified by examining some of the characteristics of one signed language, with the understanding that all signed languages, just as all spoken languages, are basically the same.

The major language used by the deaf in the United States is American Sign Language (AMESLAN or ASL). ASL is an independent, fully developed language that historically is an outgrowth of the signed language used in France and brought to the United States in 1817 by the great deaf educator Thomas Hopkins Gallaudet. Gallaudet was hired to establish a school for the deaf. After studying the language and methods used in the Paris school founded by the Abbe de l'Eppé in 1775, he returned to America with Laurent Clerc, a young deaf instructor, thus establishing the basis for ASL. But like all living languages, ASL continues to change; only 60% of the present ASL vocabulary are of French origin. Not only have new signs entered the language, but the forms of the signs have changed, in ways similar to the historical changes in the pronunciation of words in spoken language. For example, many signs that were originally formed at waist or chest level are now produced at a higher level near the neck or upper chest.

Knowing a language — spoken or signed — means knowing the *grammar* of that language. It is this kind of knowledge that Bacon was referring to. Grammar, then, is viewed by linguists as the mental system of linguistic knowledge that has been acquired by a speaker/signer which permits him or her to produce sentences and understand those produced by others, that is to express either through sounds or gestures meaningful 'utterances' which convey messages to those who can interpret these sounds or gestures.

The grammar of a language includes its 'phonology' — the sound system or visual (gestures and movements) system of that language. Phonological knowledge (which like other kinds of grammatical knowledge is often tacit or unconscious knowledge) includes the inventory of the sounds or signs which are used in that language, and knowledge of those which are not. Speakers of English, for example, unconsciously know that some of the sounds found in other languages are not part of the sound inventory of English. For example, the click sound that begins the language Xhosa, or the final sound of the name *Bach* as pronounced in German are not English sounds. Similarly, "from analyses of other signed languages, including Chinese Sign Language (Klima, Bellugi et al. 1979) it has been shown that the set of possible elements, including hand configurations, movement, and location, vary from one signed language to another" (Padden, 1988:252).

The grammar of a language includes more than the inventory of the basic minimal units of form since sequences or combinations of these basic units signify certain concepts or meanings. Knowledge of a language — one's mental grammar — thus incorporates a mental dictionary or lexicon of these meaningful units. Thus if you know English, you know the meaning of the sounds represented by the printed letters *boy* and *girl* and *language*. Similarly if you know ASL, you will relate different hand configuration and movements to different meanings (see Figure 2 below). If you do not know a language, the sounds spoken to you will be mainly incomprehensible, because the relationship between speech sounds and the meanings they represent is, for the most part, an arbitrary one. This arbitrary relationship between form and meaning is equally true in signed languages. A person who knows Chinese Sign Language would find it difficult to understand American Sign Language. Signs that may have originally been mimetic (similar to miming) or iconic (with a nonarbitrary relationship between form and meaning) change historically as do words, and the iconicity is lost. These signs become conventional; knowing the shape or movement of the hands does not reveal the meaning of the gestures in signed languages, as can be seen by the examples given in Figure 2.

Some of the words of a spoken language are composed of more than one meaningful unit (which are called *morphemes*) arranged in 'rule governed' fixed patterns, e.g. *happy* (one morpheme), *un+happy* (two morphemes) but not *happy+un*. The rules or principles in the grammar (part of the knowledge of the speakers) which determine such combinations constitute the *morphology* of the language. Sign languages have similar morphological rules. For example, in English, one can nominalize some verbs by adding the suffix -*er* e.g. *love lover, teach teacher*. In ASL, nouns can also be derived according to the morphological rules of the grammar, as can adjectives and verbs (Supalla & Newport 1978; Klima, Bellugi *et al.* 1979).

Furthermore, signs, like the morphemes and words of spoken languages, are not, as was once thought, indissoluble wholes. They can be specified by *primes* of three different sets including hand configuration, the motion of the hand(s) toward or away from the body, and the place of articulation or the locus of the sign's movement.

Figure 1 illustrates the hand configuration primes.

/B/	/A/	/G/	/C/	/5/	/V/
[B]	[A]	[G]	[C]	[5]	[V]
flat hand	fist hand	index hand	cupped hand	spread hand	V hand

/O/	/F/	/X/	/H/	/L/	/Y/
[O]	[F]	[X]	[H]	[L]	[Y]
O hand	pinching hand	hook hand	index-mid hand	L hand	Y hand

/8/	/K/	/I/	/R/	/W/	/3/	/E/
[8]	[K]	[I]	[R]	[W]	[3]	[E]
mid-finger hand	chopstick hand	pinkie hand	crossed-finger hand	American-3 hand	European-3 hand	nail-buff hand

Figure 1. Hand configuration primes arranged in order of frequency (with descriptive phrases used to refer to them).

In spoken language, two words which are distinguished phonologically by only one sound — minimal pairs — can contrast meaning, e.g. *pill* and *bill*. There are also such minimal pairs in signed languages (Figure 2) involving hand configuration, place of articulation, and movement.

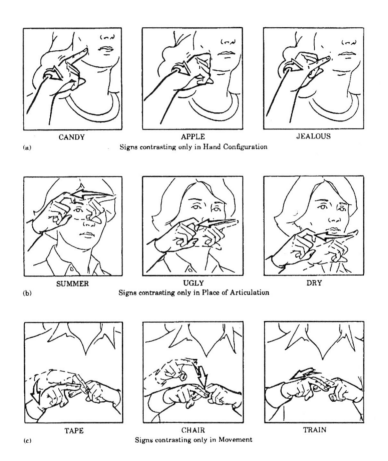

(a)   CANDY   APPLE   JEALOUS
Signs contrasting only in Hand Configuration

(b)   SUMMER   UGLY   DRY
Signs contrasting only in Place of Articulation

(c)   TAPE   CHAIR   TRAIN
Signs contrasting only in Movement

Figure 2. Minimal contrasts illustrating major formational parameters.

The sign meaning "arm" can be described as a flat hand, moving to touch the upper arm. Thus it has three prime features: flat hand, motion toward, upper arm.

Just as spoken language has sequences of sounds that are not permitted in the language, so signed languages have forbidden combinations of features. These differ from one signed language to another, just as the constraints on sounds and sound sequences differ from one spoken language to another. A permissible sign in Chinese Sign Language or Russian Sign Language may not be a permissible sign in ASL, and vice versa.

The linguistic study of ASL and other signed languages also reveals a complex system of syntactic rules that parallel those found in spoken languages. Syntax is that part of one's linguistic knowledge, the component of the mental grammar, which determines how words are to be combined to produce well-formed phrases and clauses and sentences. Neither words nor signs can be combined in any random order. There are rules for how to form questions in signed languages as well as spoken languages. Similarly, the methods for combining sentences by conjoining them or by relativization are constrained by fixed principles and rules in signed languages as they are in spoken languages.

Thus we see that there are basic universal aspects of all languages — signed and spoken. But while the basic components of the grammars of all languages are the same, the specific rules and parametric values for distinct languages differ. This is usually assumed by most people regarding the differences between spoken languages. But, because of the pervasive ignorance about signed languages, there still exists the mistaken belief that ASL consists in the replacement of each spoken English word (and morpheme) by an equivalent sign.

This word-for-word or sign-for-word translation system does exist in the United States and is called

Signed English (or Siglish). The syntax and semantics of Signed English are approximately the same as that of ordinary English. It is thus an unnatural language similar to speaking French by translating every English word or morpheme into its French counterpart. Since there is not always a morpheme or word in French that corresponds to those in English, and since French morphology and syntax is different than English morphology and syntax, this attempt at a French word-for-English word, or French morpheme-for-English morpheme translation would create serious problems just as it does in Siglish.

If there is no sign in ASL, signers utilize another mechanism, the system of fingerspelling. This is also used to add new proper nouns or technical vocabulary. Sign interpreters of spoken English often fingerspell such words. A manual alphabet consisting of various finger configurations, hand positions, and movements gives visible symbols for the alphabet and ampersand.

Signs, however, are produced differently than are fingerspelled words.

The sign DECIDE cannot be analyzed as a sequence of distinct, separable configurations of the hand. Like all other lexical signs in ASL, but unlike the individual fingerspelled letters in D-E-C-I-D-E taken separately, the ASL sign DECIDE does have an essential movement [but] [t]he handshape occurs simultaneously with the movement. In appearance, the sign is a continuous whole (Klima and Bellugi, 1979).

This is shown in Figure 3.

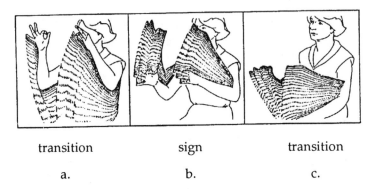

transition   sign   transition

a.   b.   c.

Figure 3. The ASL sign DECIDE. a. and c. show transitions to and from the sign; b. illustrates the single downward movement of the sign.

An accomplished signer can "speak" at a normal rate, even when there is a lot of fingerspelling, as is evidenced by watching a television program that includes a simultaneous signed interpretation in a corner of the TV screen.

Language arts are not lost to the deaf. Poetry is composed in signed language, and stage plays such as Sheridan's *The Critic* have been translated into signed language and acted by the National Theatre of the Deaf (NTD). Sign language was so highly thought of by the anthropologist Margaret Mead that, in an article discussing the possibilities of a universal second language, she suggests using some of the basic ideas that signed languages incorporate.

Given the universal aspects of signed and spoken languages, it is not surprising that deaf children of deaf signing parents parallel the stages of spoken language acquisition. They start with single signs similar to the single words in the earliest stage of spoken language acquisition and then begin to combine signs. There is also a telegraphic stage in which the "grammatical" signs — function words — are omitted. Grammatical or function signs appear at around the same age for deaf children as function words in spoken languages.

Klima and Bellugi (1979) point out that deaf children's acquisition of negation in American Sign Language (ASL) shows very much the same pattern as in spoken language. NO and NEG (a headshake) are frequently used signs in adult ASL, with different restrictions on their use. The children acquiring ASL used them interchangeably in initial position of a signed sentence, like hearing children starting negative sentences with *no* but unlike the ways in which negative signs are used in adult ASL. Thus, the acquisition of ASL cannot be simple imitation any more than spoken language is acquired simply by imitation.

Thus we see that the basic grammars of signed languages are as grammatical and systematic as are spoken languages; signs are as conventional or arbitrary as are the words of spoken language. Since all languages change in time, just as there are many different spoken languages, there are many different signed languages, all of which (spoken and signed) reveal the same linguistic universals. Deaf children often sign themselves to sleep just as hearing children talk themselves to sleep; deaf children report that they dream in signed language as French speaking children dream in French, and Hopi children dream in Hopi and American children dream in English. Deaf children sign to their dolls and stuffed animals; slips of the hand occur and are similar to slips of the tongue; finger fumblers amuse signers as do tongue twisters amuse speakers. We see that signed languages resemble spoken languages in all major aspects, showing that there truly are universals of language despite differences in the modality in which the language is performed. This is predictable because it is language, not speech, which is biologically based.

References

Fromkin, V.A. 1985. Implications of hemispheric differences for linguistics. In *The Dual Brain*, edited by D.Frank Benson and Eran Zaidel. New York: The Guilford Press, 319-327.

Fromkin, V.A. 1988. The state of brain/language research. In *Language, Communication, and the Brain*. Edited by Fred Plum. New York: The Raven Press, 1-18.

Fromkin, V.A. & Rodman, R. 1988. *An Introduction to Language* (Fourth Edition). New York: Holt, Rinehart and Winston.

Geschwind, N. 1979. Specializations of the human brain. *Scientific American* 206: 180-199.

Klima, E.S. Klima & U. Bellugi. 1979. *The Signs of Language*. Cambridge, Mass.: Harvard University Press.

Padden, Carol A. 1988. Grammatical theory and signed languages. In *Linguistics: The Cambridge Survey II*. Edited by Frederick J. Newmeyer. Cambridge and New York: Cambridge University Press, 250-266.

The Culture of American Deaf People

Susan D. Rutherford
University of California, Berkeley

When the issue of accepting American Sign Language (ASL) to meet a foreign language requirement is raised, it is often followed with questions such as: Does ASL have a culture? Is there a literature? Aren't its users simply a subculture? Does it meet the intent of a humanities requirement? This is not surprising because the idea of ASL being a complete and sophisticated language is relatively new to academic literature and is just beginning to be popularly known. Further, seeing Deaf people as a cultural entity instead of as isolated people with impaired hearing challenges the greater American society's perception about Deaf people — this is the cultural matrix in which even academia finds itself. Responses from this perception are often negative toward the language and thus its people. This paper seeks to address these questions and perceptions, and hopes to provide illumination on why we can say, yes, there is an American Deaf culture; that there is much students can learn about humanity in general and themselves in particular from the study of ASL; and that it is a legitimate field of inquiry for "foreign" language study worthy of our attention and support.

The Nature of Culture

To begin, let us quickly review the nature of culture. As a species, homo sapiens is particularly dependent at birth and continues this dependent status for a prolonged period of time. We cannot feed ourselves, we are not mobile, and we have very little idea or understanding of the world that we have just entered. To survive we need to be fed, sheltered, and educated. The mechanism that provides this and thus ensures the survival of the species is culture. Culture is transmitted and learned through language. Language is learned within the context of culture — thus, language and culture are inextricably bound. It is culture that has kept us at the top of the phylogenetic scale despite our helpless and rather pathetic status at birth relative to others of the animal world. It is our facility with language that makes us uniquely human.

Culture is a design for living (Geertz, 1973). It consists of whatever one has to know or believe in order to operate in a manner acceptable to its members (Goodenough, 1970). It tells a people what their needs are and how to go about meeting those needs. It is the shared experience, knowledge, and values of the group.

There is a wide variety and variance in cultural knowledge and behaviors across humankind. Despite this appearance of dissimilarity among the societies of the world, however, all cultures share two primary objectives. One is the successful adaptation and survival of the group in its specific environment; the other is the maintenance of the group's identity and unity through time.

That there are so many different kinds of environments to adapt to accounts in large measure for the amount of diversity we see in the cultures of the world. For example, the adaptation to climate by the Eskimo in the North American Arctic is quite different from the adaptation to climate by the Yanamamo of tropical Brazil. The climate and available resources determine the food, shelter, and clothing of each group. Where resources are marginal culture instills behaviors and traditions that ensure the survival of the group, whether it is survival in an African desert or Nordic tundra. Culture passes on the knowledge to the Kung! Bushmen of the Kalahari of which roots contain water during the dry season and to the Arctic Skolt Lapps of how to raise and herd reindeer.

These examples of culture working as an adaptive mechanism to the environment have focused on illustrations that are easy to understand and have been widely studied. Because these are the sorts of examples often used, we tend to think that culture only belongs to semi-clad natives appearing in the pages of National Geographic. Americans tend not to conceive of culture as an adaptive mechanism in our own industrialized society. Perhaps contributing to this notion is the fact that American anthropologists have traditionally studied other cultures, not our own. This is no doubt a legacy of the British founders of the discipline who set out to study "primitive" peoples.

The goal of anthropology is the understanding of humankind. Consistent with this goal it is fortunate that the pejorative attitude toward studying the culture of Americans is beginning to change. We can learn much about humankind and its adaptation in industrial societies too. In fact, with the increased concentration on industrializing the Third World, this knowledge may prove critical in understanding the new adaptive needs of these people. I mention this as part of the intellectual backdrop that exists when we find resistance to the idea of a Deaf culture. People tend to think that only those cultures which are seen as foreign are valid for serious study. Further, when we say that culture is an adaptation to an environment, we often think that environment refers only to such things as climate and available resources. Environment, however, refers to the total circumstances and conditions in which a people find themselves — the entire milieu. This includes climate and resources; it also includes an environment that is void of usable sound.

The Deaf Adaptation

The culture of Deaf people is an adaptation to such an environment. I say usable sound not to imply that all Deaf people cannot hear sound, but that the environment is void of the range of sound that encompasses speech. This is drawing from our society's definitions of "deaf" meaning the inability to perceive the sounds of speech. This is a critical distinction, because the environment then dictates a need to develop a language not based on a sound system. The major boundary of the culture is thus created by this environmental constraint.

To be social one must have a language. For a person to live outside of a social group is not to exist. We are social beings. It is our language that gives us an identity, a means by which we learn about the world, what is real and not real, right and not right, who we are and who we are not.

It is obvious that for people who find themselves in
an environment void of the very sound that is the access to an aural language, the most fundamental and
primary human adaptation will be the evolution of a
language whose building blocks are suitable. In the
case of the world's Deaf cultures the adaptation is visual.

Indeed, what makes Deaf people a cultural group
instead of simply a loose organization of people with a
similar sensory loss is the fact that their adaptation includes language. An environment created solely by a
sensory deprivation does not make a culture. Blind
people find themselves in a visual void. This similarity
in circumstance certainly provides for a strong group
bonding of individuals of similar experience; it does
not, however, form a culture. Blind people are vision-
impaired members of the variety of Americas' linguistic communities. What does form a culture for Deaf
people is the fact that the adaptation to a visual world
has by human necessity included a visual language. In
the United States this is American Sign Language.

The Language

ASL is not derivative of any oral language but like
oral languages it has a unique phonological, syntactic,
and semantic structure. It has the creative flexibility
necessary to develop new vocabulary and new grammatical structures (Friedman, 1977:13–56). It serves the
same social and intellectual functions as spoken languages. It is not a universal language. Others of the
world's Deaf cultures have their own unique visual
languages.

Historically, ASL is related to French Sign Language (FSL), which was introduced into the United States in the early nineteenth century by a French Deaf educator, Laurent Clerc, and the Reverend Thomas Gallaudet, who together founded the American Asylum for the Deaf in Hartford, Connecticut. There the FSL mixed with the indigenous American signed languages to form the roots of today's ASL (Woodward and Erting, 1975). Approximately 60% of today's ASL contains FSL cognates. Although they have grown in separate directions in their respective cultures since the early 1800's, ASL and FSL are still somewhat mutually intelligible, similar to spoken Spanish and Italian. FSL and ASL have developed independently from French and English and are not even remotely similar in structure to these spoken languages. Theoretically, an American student of ASL could carry on a rudimentary conversation with a French student of FSL without either of them having any knowledge of the spoken language of the other. The signed language used in Great Britain also developed independently of spoken English. In fact, unlike the spoken languages in England and the United States, British Sign Language and American Sign Language are not related historically nor are they mutually intelligible (Friedman, 1977:3).

American Sign Language, like all spoken languages, has its regional dialects and slang. It is a unique, living, evolving language and is not a manual code for English. It is used by people, as is any of the world's languages, "to interact with each other, to communicate their ideas, emotions and intentions, and to transmit their culture from generation to generation" (Baker and Cokely, 1980:31).

Cultural Characteristics

The core of the American Deaf culture is ASL, and its use is the chief identifying characteristic of membership in the Deaf community. The community is comprised of deaf and hard-of-hearing individuals who share this common language, common experiences, and common values (Baker and Padden, 1978). They share a common way of interacting with each other and with the hearing world. The Deaf community does not include all people who are deaf. In the United States there are over two million people who are audiometrically deaf, that is, who are physically unable to perceive the sounds of speech. The American Deaf community, however, numbers approximately 500,000. Membership in this cultural group is based more on "attitudinal deafness" than on the actual degree of hearing loss. As Baker and Padden (1978:4) explain, attitudinal deafness means that an individual has, on the basis of certain characteristics, identified him/herself as a member of the community and is accepted by the other members. This process parallels Barth's (1969) suggestion on the formation of ethnic groups where membership is determined by an individual's identification with the group and by the group, in turn, recognizing and identifying the individual as a member. Because the use of American Sign Language is the major identifying characteristic of members of the Deaf community, individuals who are deaf but do not use ASL are not considered members of the cultural group (for further discuss see Baker and Battison, 1980; Woodward, 1982; Meadow, 1972; Markowicz and Woodward, 1975; Rutherford, 1987, and Lunde, 1960).

In addition to having a language that identifies its
members, the community has other cultural characteristics that are well documented, such as its 85 to 95 percent endogamous marriage rate (Rainier, Altschuler,
and Kallman, 1963; Schein and Delk, 1974; Fay, 1898).
Deaf people tend to marry other Deaf people exclusively. Still another characteristic, the existence of a formal societal structure within the culture, can be seen in
the numerous Deaf organizations — local, state, national, and international. Of particular note are the National Association of the Deaf (est. 1880) and the World
Federation of the Deaf (est. 1951), which involve themselves with the problems of the deaf in national and international levels. There is an American Athletic
Association of the Deaf, which organizes Deaf sports
and, since 1935, has assisted American participation in
the World Deaf Olympics. This year's games, for example, will be held in Christchurch, New Zealand. Finally, there are national fraternal orders, sororities, and
alumni associations, as well as numerous religious organizations and community social groups (for further
discussion, see Meadow, 1972; Jacobs, 1981; Gannon,
1981).

Articles of material culture specific to the community also exist, such as telecommunication devices that
enable telephone communication, and flashing light
signaling devices to take the place of doorbells, clock
alarms, and telephone rings. There are even sound-ac-
tivated signal lights to alert parents to a baby's cry. The
culture has developed many devices and behaviors to
adapt to the physical world. In fact, the Smithsonian
has a collection which includes artifacts from before
the advent of electricity, such as door knockers made

from a cannonball attached to a rope. A visitor would pull on the rope outside the door, which would cause the cannonball to bounce repeatedly on the floor inside. The vibrations would call the attention of the Deaf person to the door. (Maybe such a device is best called a floor knocker.) Regardless, the invention of adaptive devices did not dawn with the advent of electricity, but has been a part of Deaf culture through time.

All of the above characteristics — marriage patterns, societal structure, and material artifacts — define the group, but again, nothing so much as the language. Roughly 10 percent of the Deaf community's population are members of Deaf families whose principal language is ASL. The remaining approximately 90 percent of the population are born to hearing families and are consequently potential members of a different cultural group from their own parents. It is a unique characteristic of this cultural group that many of its members acquire the group's primary trait, language, not from parents but from peers. State-operated residential schools for the deaf are the primary places where enculturation of these children takes place (Meadow, 1972:24; Nash, 1987). There, through peers from Deaf families and through a Deaf adult staff, if any are present, the transmission of culture and language takes place. For the majority of the population the residential school is where the process of identification with a Deaf group begins.

Deaf Identity

In addition to providing mechanisms for adapting to a visual world, the culture of American Deaf people also provides for the maintenance of the group's identity and integrity through time.

Let us return to the environment that Deaf people find themselves in and to which they must adapt. It is an environment where the majority culture often sees only the deafness, the pathology of the individual, and not the cultural identity of the group's members. Deaf people are generally seen as isolated, impaired individuals within this society. Rarely is the Deaf individual viewed as an intact, healthy Deaf person who is a member of a larger cultural entity. There is a rich legacy of cultural traditions and customs, norms and values, history and folklore, literature and art that serve in the maintenance of the identity and solidarity of the group (for further discussion see Rutherford, 1987).

Deaf people with a positive Deaf identity see themselves as whole Deaf persons. With this self-esteem intact, the Deaf individual has a strong base of identity from which to venture into and negotiate the hearing world. One does not have to be an anthropologist or educator to see the adaptive nature of culture here and how it fosters the survival of the group and its members. The culture itself provides the requisite identity and attendant esteem necessary for learning and interacting with the world as a fully functioning human being.

This cultural identity is intrinsically bound to the language. When the Northern and Southern soldiers in a Deaf Civil War legend signed what could be glossed as DEAF-SAME, it was not an affirmation of a mutual lack of hearing, but rather one of mutual identity. In fact, in this legend which continues to be told, it is an identity that transcended North and South allegiances (Rutherford, 1987).

Literature

The study of American Deaf culture has shown distinct differences between that culture and the mainstream society in social attitude, patterns for daily living, world view, humor, and literature. This last is important because some critics have questioned whether there is a body of literature of the culture. The ASL literary output consists of a wealth of materials in a variety of genres, including works of ASL history, stories, poetry, plays, and folklore in print, videotape, and film formats. (For further discussion see Gannon, 1981; Lane, 1984; Groce, 1980; Miles, 1975; Klima and Bellugi, 1975, 1979; Eastman, 1974; Bragg and Bergman, 1981; Rutherford, 1983, 1984, 1985, 1987.) The folkloristic tradition of Deaf America is over 175 years old and is replete with legends, naming practices, tall tales, folkspeech, jokes, sign play, games, folk poetry, customs, ritual, and celebrations (Rutherford, 1984, 1987; Carmel, 1980). There are published works created by Deaf playwrights that reflect the Deaf experience on stage such as A Play of Our Own by Dorothy Miles; Sign Me Alice by Gilbert Eastman; and Tales from a Clubroom by Bernard Bragg and Eugene Bergman, and novels such as Islay by Douglas Bullard.

There are Deaf publishers whose primary focus is the publication of Deaf literature and related materials in print and electronic media. Among them are T.J. Publishers, Inc.; Dawn Sign Press, Inc.; National Association of the Deaf; and Gallaudet University Press. Linstok Press, Inc. focuses on scholarly publication.

Mainstream publishers, including Harvard University Press, University of California Press, University of Illinois Press, Alfred A. Knopf, and Random House, among many others, have published major works on Deaf culture and literature and are becoming increasingly interested in the field. National publishers focusing primarily on videotape and film production of works in ASL include D.E.A.F. Media, Inc., Sign Media, Inc., and Beyond Sound, Inc. Other producers of ASL videotape materials include Gallaudet University, the National Technical Institute for the Deaf, and the San Francisco Public Library.

The Visual Arts

In addition to literature and folklore, the Deaf community has, as one might imagine, a long tradition in the visual arts. Oil portraits by John Brewster (1766–1854), who was one of the original students of the American Asylum for the Deaf, hand in Williamsburg. Etching of Cadwallader L. Washburn (1866–1965) are world renowned. Works by Washburn, David Block (1910–), Robert J. Freiman (1917–), Felix Kowalewski (1913–), and Morris Broderson (1928–), to name a few, have hung in the Metropolitan Museum of Art in New York, The National Gallery in Washington, D.C., the Boston Museum of Fine Arts, Carnegie Institute, and the San Francisco Palace of Fine Arts (Gannon, 1981; 93–156). Monumental works by sculptor Douglas Tilden (1860–1935) are prominent parts of the San Francisco Bay Area public landscape with works in Golden Gate Park, on the University of California campus, and in prominent locations on downtown Market Street. The work of art historian, Dr. Deborah Sonnenstrahl, and doctoral candidate, Paul Johnston, both of Gallaudet University, continues to document the history of Deaf artists. Deaf Artists of America, a newly formed national organization, also is working in this endeavor.

The art of a society is usually an accurate and clear representation of a culture's values and beliefs. The following poignant work by Betty G. Miller is a prime example of Deaf art reflecting its culture. Titled "Ameslan Prohibited" (1972) it dramatically exhibits the feeling of a people toward the suppression of their language.

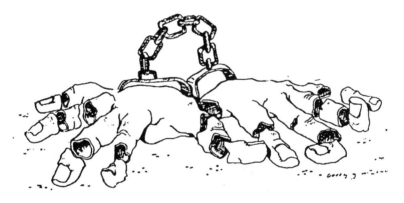

The Bilingual/Bicultural Community

As with all cultural groups who desire participation and self-determination in American society, the use of the majority language, English, is necessary. As such, most Deaf Americans are bilingual and bicultural to a variety of degrees. This situation is perhaps best described by Kannapel (1974:9–15) in her "Proposed Classifications of Deaf Children and Adults" as follows:

ASL Monolinguals. They are comfortable expressing themselves only in ASL and understanding ASL.

ASL-Dominant Bilinguals. They are comfortable
expressing themselves in ASL better than in English and are able to understand ASL better than
English (in either printed or signed form).

Balanced Bilinguals. They are comfortable expressing themselves in both ASL and English
about equally well.

English-Dominant Bilinguals. They are comfortable expressing themselves in English and are
able to understand English (in printed and signed
form) better than ASL.

English Monolinguals. They are comfortable expressing themselves only in English (in oral or
signed English) and understanding English (in
printed or oral or signed English).

It is very much a part of Deaf culture that members
must adjust to different situations — dealing with
hearing people, with orally-trained deaf people, and so
on. The Deaf person, therefore, functions day-to-day at
various points along a diglossic continuum, code-
switching among language varieties unconsciously as
the situation demands (Stokoe, 1970; Woodward,
1978).

Deaf Culture as an American Subculture

Culture in the American context is not one singular,
integrated culture, but more a mosaic of a variety of
cultures largely held together by the majority societal
economic, political, educational, and legal systems.

The American Deaf community is one of the cultures in this grand mosaic. In pluralistic societies such as ours, subcultural variation is particularly marked. We use the term "subculture" to refer to a group of people within the culture who have formulated a way of behaving that includes some of the dominant features of the cultural average but also includes certain features not found elsewhere in the society. This term thus defined can be used to refer to a wide range of groups within American society. A subculture in this sense can refer to an occupational group, such as doctors or soldiers; to regional groups such as Southerners or Texans; and to groups as diverse a seniors, drug addicts, and teenagers. It can also refer to linguistic groups such as Chinese, French, or Italian. All of these groups are subcultures in relationship to the larger American society, and it is appropriate to use the term in referring to all of them. The latter, however, by virtue of having an identity based in a separate and different language and culture, are certainly qualitatively different from the former. It is unfortunate that the term subculture with its prefix "sub" has a negative connotation and implies something qualitatively less. The negative impression is especially hard on groups whose language may be appropriate for study as foreign languages. Where it would be inappropriate to study the language of subcultures such as American teenagers, Texans, or the military to meet a foreign language requirement, the same cannot be said of the culture of American Deaf people. As a linguistic subculture which is a culture in its own right, the American Deaf community (and this, American Sign Language) is as appropriate a subject to study as any foreign culture that may also be an American subculture, e.g. Italian, Spanish, French, Chinese, and so forth.

The Enduring Culture

Many writers have noted that throughout history, communities have considered their language to be their most precious possession for it contained their cultural heritage and identity. Gottfried Herder, for example, once commented that language is the possession held most dear among a group of people because in it "resides its whole thought domain, its tradition, history, religion, and basis of life, all its heart and soul." To deprive a people of its language, Herder wrote, "is to deprive it of its one eternal good" (quoted by Fishman, 1972:1).

The Deaf community is no different. In response to what it saw as a fearful trend — a kind of linguistic genocide — the National Association of the Deaf (NAD) in 1913 initiated a film project for the preservation of sign language. In his presentation titled "The Preservation of the Sign Language" George W. Veditz, the then-president of the NAD, stated:

> 'A new race of pharaohs that knew not Joseph' is not taking over the land and many of our American schools. They do not understand signs for they cannot sign. They proclaim that signs are worthless and of no help to the deaf. Enemies of sign language, they are enemies of the true welfare of the Deaf. We must, with various films, protect and pass on our beautiful signs as we now have them.

The film project continued until 1920, recording some of the more active bearers of the traditions of

Deaf people and those whose signing was esteemed as the most eloquent. It is a rich resource for study today. It also serves as a reminder of the long history of linguistic oppression that Deaf people have endured. The "pharaohs" of 1913 "that knew not Joseph" did not recognize American Sign Language nor did they recognize Deaf people as a people — both of which has led to much suffering (see Lane, 1984; Jacobs, 1981). This was not because they were hateful hearing people imposing their ill will on the Deaf, but rather because they were products of an education system and a society that was ignorant of the facts. With its long history of being overtly oppressed, the fact that ASL survives today is living testimony to the strength of its culture. This strength is witnessed in the resolve of the film's emphatic closing statement by Veditz, "As long as we have Deaf people on earth, we will have signs ..."

Deaf Studies

For the anthropologist and the student of language this is a remarkable example to study. It opens new realms for the study of language, its acquisition, transmission, history of development, relationship to culture, and the very nature of human adaptation.

For students of ASL there is this and more. Students are able to gain a greater sensitivity to and understanding of another culture with different perceptions and world view. They expand their understanding of the interrelationship between the creative arts, the humanities, and the self. They become more aware of their own language and culture. This major goal of universities' foreign language requirements seems, in my ten years teaching experience, to come into quicker and sharper focus for the hearing student of ASL because the visual modality of the language is so unlike the spoken languages they know.

As academics we are mandated with the responsibility of expanding the realm of knowledge. Those of us on curriculum committees also have a particular responsibility to be prudent in this endeavor. We are poised at a point in the history of this field where we have documentation attesting to the legitimacy of the language and culture of Deaf people. We have an expanding body of literature reflecting the richness of their history, ideas, values, traditions, and world view. We have a long-established tradition in the creative arts — performing and visual. We also have a rare situation where we can offer a language and cultural group that our students can study first-hand in their own backyard. We have responsible curriculum and materials developed in keeping with our most current scholarship on language teaching (see Smith elsewhere in this issue). And we have increased research on other signed languages of the world, offering the chance for comparative study. In short, we have the rare opportunity to formally recognize a fully functioning cultural group and, at the same time, to open the doors for our students to rich new fields of intellectual inquiry.

References

Baker, C. & R. Battison, Eds. 1980. *Sign Language and the Deaf Community — Essays in Honor of William C. Stokoe.* Silver Spring, MD: National Association of the Deaf.

Baker, C. & D. Cokely. 1980. *American Sign Language: A Teacher's Resource Text on Grammar and Culture.* Silver Spring, MD: T.J. Publishers, Inc.

Baker, C. & C. Padden. 1978. *American Sign Language: A Look at its History, Structure, and Community.* Silver Spring, MD: T.J. Publishers, Inc.

Barth, F. 1969. *Ethnic Groups and Boundaries.* Boston: Little, Brown.

Bragg, B. & E. Bergman. 1981. *Tales from a Clubroom.* Washington, DC: Gallaudet University Press.

Bullard, D. 1985. *Islay.* Silver Spring, MD: T.J. Publishers, Inc.

Carmel, S. 1980. *Deaf Folklore.* Video produced by Gallaudet University Television.

Eastman, G. 1974. *Sign Me Alice.* Washington, DC: Gallaudet University Press.

Fay, E.A. 1898. *Marriages of the Deaf in America.* Washington, DC: Volta Bureau.

Fishman, J. A. 1972. *Language and Nationalism: Two Integrative Essays.* Rowley, MA: Newbury House.

Friedman, L. A. 1977. Formational Properties of American Sign Language. In L. A. Friedman (ed.), *On the Other Hand: New Perspectives on American Sign Language.* NY: Academic Press.

Gannon, J. R. 1981. *Deaf Heritage: A Narrative History of Deaf America.* Silver Spring, MD: National Association of the Deaf.

Geertz, C. 1973. *The Interpretation of Culture.* NY: Basic Books.

Goodenough, W. H. 1970. *Description and Comparison in Cultural Anthropology*. Chicago: Aldine.

Groce, N. 1980. Everyone Here Spoke Sign Language. *Natural History, 89(6)*, 10–16.

Jacobs, L. M. 1981. *A Deaf Adult Speaks Out*. Washington, DC: Gallaudet University Press.

Kannapell, B. 1974. Bilingualism: A New Direction in the Education of the Deaf. *The Deaf American, 26,* 9–15.

Klima, E. & U. Bellugi. 1979. *The Signs of Language*. Cambridge, MA: Harvard University Press.

Klima, E. & U. Bellugi. 1975. Wit and Poetry in American Sign Language. *Sign Language Studies, 8*, 203–224.

Lane, H. 1984. *When the Mind Hears*. NY: Random House.

Lunde, A. 1960. The Sociology of the Deaf. In W. Stokoe, *Sign Language Structure: An Outline of Visual Communication Systems of the American Deaf*. University of Buffalo: Occassional Paper 8.

Markowicz, H. & J. Woodward. 1975. Language and the Maintenance of Ethnic Boundaries in the Deaf Community. *Communication and Cognition, 11*, 29–38.

Meadow, K. 1972. Sociolinguistics, Sign Language and the Deaf Subculture. In T.J. O'Rourke (ed.), *Psycholinguistics and Total Communication: The State of the Art*. Silver Spring, MD: American Annal of the Deaf.

Miles, D. 1976. *Gestures:* Poetry by Dorothy Miles. Northridge, CA: Joyce Motion Picture Co.

Nash, J. E. 1987. Policy and Practice in the American Sign Language Community. *International Journal of the Sociology of Language, 68, 7–22.*

Rainer, J., Altschuler, K. & F. Kallman, Eds. 1963. *Family and Mental Health Problems in a Deaf Population.* NY: Department of Genetics, New York State Psychiatric Institute, Columbia University.

Rutherford, S. D. 1983. Funny in Deaf — Not in Hearing. *Journal of American Folklore.* Washington, DC: American Folklore Society, 310–322.

Rutherford, S.D. 1984. *Deaf Heritage; Deaf Folklore; Deaf Literature; Deaf Minorities.* American Culture: The Deaf Perspective. Video series produced for the National Endowment of the Humanities by the San Francisco Public Library.

Rutherford, S.D. 1985. The Traditional Group Narrative of Deaf Children. *Sign Language Studies, 47,* 141–159.

Rutherford, S.D. 1987. *A Study of American Deaf Folklore.* Unpublished Doctoral Dissertation, University of California, Berkeley.

Schein, J. and M. Delk. 1974. *The Deaf Population of the United States.* Silver Spring, MD: National Association of the Deaf.

Stokoe, W. C. 1970. Sign Language Diglossia. *Studies in Linguistics, 21,* 27–41.

Woodward, J. 1973. "Some Observations on Sociolinguistic Variation and American Sign Language." *Kansas Journal of Sociology, 9,* 191–199.

Woodward, J. 1982.*How You Gonna Get to Heaven If You Can't Talk With Jesus: The Educational Establishment vs. The Deaf Community.* Silver Spring, MD: T.J. Publishers, Inc.

Signers of Tales: The Case for Literary Status of an Unwritten Language

Nancy Frishberg
IBM Corporation

One of the most frequently cited arguments against granting academic credit for courses in American Sign Language (ASL) continues to be the presumed "lack of literature." Chapin's introduction to this volume gives us two recent cases. My own experience in dealing with curriculum committees in several major universities has given me a chance to confront skeptical colleagues face-to-face. I wish I could report that my successes were universal. In fact, they have been limited. I have managed to aid several graduate students in getting ASL accepted for their foreign language reading or competency requirement. I have helped create additional exceptional cases for undergraduates, like the one cited in Chapin (above). In the interest of affecting attitudes of even more skeptics and aiding colleagues engaged in similar efforts, the following remarks collect the arguments refuting ASL's "lack of literature" and will propose several curricular remedies to improve those sign language courses which suffer from inadequate focus on literary traditions of the deaf.

A bit more background may give insight. In the early years of this decade I was invited to participate in a
unique curricular partnership. The Theater Department and the Education Department of a local undergraduate program wanted to highlight their strengths
together. They asked me to help them make their well-
known children's theater productions accessible to
deaf audiences by involving the students enrolled in
deaf education, theirs being the only B.A. program in
deaf education resulting in state certified teachers in
the city. For several years (1982–1985), I taught a course
for Marymount Manhattan College (New York, NY)
called "Sign Language and the Performing Arts." I
asked that this course be required of students audition-
ing for roles as student interpreters in the spring children's theater productions. It was my belief then, as
now, that students with a limited exposure to sign language should gain a bit of perspective on their place in
the literary lives of their audience. The deaf students
who would see our productions might never have attended a live theatrical performance before, nor have
been exposed to interpreters, but these facts did not
mean that their lives up until now had been lacking in
structured or traditional forms of performance, nor
that they would not be exposed to even more language
art in their own language. The deaf adults whom we
would invite to attend the performances would come
with rich experiences of deaf theater, interpreted performances, and a variety of verbal art forms. The following remarks, then, have grown out of this course, as
well as prior reflections on what constitutes a traditional and conventional verbal art form in a language without sound or writing.

Defining a literary aesthetic

Does a literary tradition depend on a written tradition? This question may be crucial for some who argue against ASL's academic status because of literature. I believe the case can be made by analogy with the greatest traditions in Western and non-Western literature that written forms of language are not required for a community to possess a well-formed aesthetic in poetry, narrative, humor, and rhetoric.

Greek and Balkan Epics. Consider, first, the classical Greek Odyssey: it is without question a literary work worthy of study by students of Greek language, and in translation by students of literature. Can we assume that its author wrote the tale down himself, or even that there was a single person called Homer? Albert Lord argues convincingly that Homer "represents all singers of tales from time immemorial and unrecorded to the present. Each [of whom...] is as much a part of the tradition of oral epic singing as is Homer" (1964:vii). Lord cites the evidence that the epics we know today as classics of ancient Greek literature must have been passed on orally for a long time before being written down, that writing only came to the languages of that part of the world well after the events depicted in the tale would have taken place. Nonetheless, this epic forms the heart of Western literary traditions.

Its poetic structure is apparently shared with other, more recent, Balkan tales. Lord goes on to argue that oral epic song is narrative poetry composed by people who didn't know how to write. It consists of metrical lines and half lines using formulas which are not frozen forms, but are rather productive words or phrases that fit given metrical conditions (4). In fact, Lord has studied the oral epics generated by skilled "singers of tales" in Yugoslavia from roughly 1945–55. The modern examples of Balkan epic poetic exhibit the strict adherence to meter, rhyme, imagery, and narrative cohesion that we find in studying the ancient written example more familiar to us. The differences are that the modern forms are spoken rather than written, composed in performance at rapid rates of production. Lord argues that it is this speed of composition that forces the use of formulaic and traditional elements.

The distinction here must be drawn between oral literature as pure oral memorization and oral composition. While less skilled singers may learn a few songs or verses through memorization, the singer with a more representative repertoire of 30 or more epic songs will not rely on memorization. Lord's detailed analysis shows just how elements are rearranged, how metrical structure interacts with grammar and meaning. His study concentrates on not only how the performers compose, but also how they learn and transmit their epics (vii).

Having dismissed rote memorization, let us not swing to the opposite conclusion: the epics are not broad improvisation, but rather are improvised within the restrictions of a particular style. The metrical types and rhyming patterns fit a closely held traditional form. While individual singers have distinct and identifiable styles, the genre of oral epic poetry holds the reins on totally unbounded improvisation.

Thus, we see that the very foundation of Western literary traditions has its roots in an oral narrative tradition, one which is still alive today. The restriction of "literature" to that which is written down denies the shared aesthetic common to both modes of presentation, oral and written. The notions of meter, rhythm, rhyme, image, and other poetic devices are constant irrespective of mode. We should not artificially limit ourselves to those examples of language art which can be studied via the written page.

Yiddish. Isaac Bashevis Singer received the Nobel Prize for Literature in 1978 honoring his literary output in Yiddish. In his remarks, he said, "The high honor bestowed upon me by the Swedish Academy is also a recognition of the Yiddish language — a language of exile, without a land, without frontiers, not supported by any government, a language which possesses no words for weapons, ammunition, military exercises, war tactics; a language that was despised by both gentiles and emancipated Jews." (6–7) His writing and the acknowledgment of his prolific and accomplished literary output through this prize focused world attention on a long but largely unknown literary tradition of Yiddish newspapers, plays, romantic novels, and works translated from other great languages of the world.

Although writing in Yiddish has been known for nearly 1000 years, efforts to elevate that writing to full public status were hampered for many years, even centuries, because of several factors. Yiddish is written using Hebrew characters. Structurally the language was originally the German spoken in Jewish communities of the Rhineland; in subsequent generations it has grown as Jewish communities came in contact with various other languages, Polish, Russian, Hungarian, French, Latvian, English among others. The first Yiddish writing was literature in translation, sometimes adapted to remove non-Jewish religious references. So the Nibelungenlied and the stories of King Arthur reached Jewish audiences from the 15th century onward.

Yiddish lacked authority, however, since the community recognized Hebrew alone as the language of law, of official records (both religious and otherwise), and naturally of religious practice. Yiddish might be fine for non-serious purposes, such as writing romances, quasi-religious or ethical teachings aimed at a female audience, namely that audience which was not expected or required to read Hebrew. In the past century, scholarly attention has been drawn to the linguistic description of Yiddish structure and dialect variants, the preservation and criticism of Yiddish literature and the teaching of Yiddish language to adults. YIVO, the Yiddish institute, is dedicated to these several goals, but interestingly it was only founded in 1925. During the discussions of the founding of a Jewish state, Yiddish partisans attempted to make it the official language of world Jewry. In fact, efforts to modernize biblical Hebrew won out, and the Holocaust of World War II destroyed more than half the world's Yiddish speakers (Gittleman, 1978:11-21).

The comparison with ASL and other deaf sign languages is particularly apt. For deaf signers, only within the past 25 years has their language won the respect of scholarly scrutiny. Cohn's indictment of earlier efforts of deaf poets cites the borrowed aesthetic of auditory rhyme and spoken language meter (264). The movement away from literature in translation alone to narrative, poetry, theater composed from within the deaf sign language itself is either relatively recent, or the artifacts are more available and appreciated by the wider signing audience than ever before. Furthermore, deaf authors, poets, and playwrights are composing from impulses within the Deaf cultural tradition. The examples cited below show the importance of the deaf social club, the constant conflict for the right to "speak" for oneself using the language of one's own, the role of the residential school in developing social values and imparting more than schoolbook education.

Non-Western Traditions. Without belaboring the point, the case could equally well be made for literature among the peoples of Polynesia whose oral recitations of genealogical history are well-known, and among the Aborigines of Australia, whose poetic traditions refer extensively to dreamtime, a prehistory, in which the moral and ethical culture was set forth. Neither of these traditions relies on written language; both involve traditional language forms used within a highly stylized cultural context.

Gary Witherspoon (1977) shows us that the traditional healing ceremonies of the Navajo are built on a foundation of culturally understood relationships between thought, speech, language, and knowledge. That is, the Navajo philosophical framework motivates the traditions of ritual, including the parts of ritual involving language.

Writing down language

Alternatively, some critics may claim that since it is not generally possible to write signs down adequately, the lack of a writing system should indict the literary study of this language.[1] Let us not confuse form for substance. There do exist several proposals for orthographic systems for signs, including the notation of William Stokoe's important and useful *Dictionary of ASL on Linguistics Principles* (1965, 1980) and Valerie Sutton's (1982) adaptation of her dance notation. Instructors who feel comfortable with any of these may find it a useful tool to attune students' analytic eyes to the fine details of signs. Other instructors may accomplish the same goals by alternative means. The conventions for transcribing ASL signs using capitalized English words (to distinguish a gloss from a full translation) with additional diacritical markings have been introduced by several of the more popular textbook authors (cf. Baker & Cokely 1980), and students become accustomed to these conventions after a few class meetings and home study sessions.

Albert Lord, in his already cited "The Singer of Tales," describes the relationship between writing or transcribing the songs and their performance. For many accomplished singers, the process involved in reciting at a pace slow enough for transcription into written form deforms or disturbs the performance. The usual rapid pace of composition might measure 10–20 ten-syllable lines per minute (17). What's more, writing down an oral epic fixes it for the world of literates. It does not change the epic for the author-performer, who continues to take that as one instance of a recitation of that song. But for the world of written language and literature, that instance becomes *the* song (124–5).

Alternative recording techniques (other than manual transcription of a live performance) are now avail-

---

[1] Scribner and Cole (1981) discuss alternative functions for three writing systems that coexist in one Liberian speech community.

able through advances in video and audio recording, alternatives which are less intrusive to the performance. In addition, we find greater general availability of devices to play back performances recorded by these means. I submit that access to videotape and film can permit pedagogical approaches to understanding traditional forms in American Sign Language.

In short, the lack of writing tradition should not stand in the way of our discovering literary traditions, in the ways language users store and share their common understandings of the world's wisdom and mysteries.

Deaf people who share a community have shared ways of expressing their understandings of the world, their values and beliefs, the lore of being different in a potentially hostile and frequently foolish world, and of recognizing language as an object of beauty and play. Some of these understandings have begun to be analyzed by academics. Some of the same ones and others can be found in film and videotape resources, which have proved valuable supplements to texts, classroom discussions, and community involvement.

ASL Genres

I have found three indigenous major genres of literature in ASL. (I assume a similar case can be made for most of the sign languages with which I am familiar, especially those of Western Europe, Asia, and the Soviet Union.) The three primary genres are that of oratory, folklore, and performance art. In some respects these are artificial boundaries, useful more for analytic purposes than any other reason. The following descriptions are not intended to exhaustively identify

particular settings or sub-types within these three
genres, but rather to give the reader sufficient evidence
to support the division into three.

Oratory

The first recordings of ASL on film document the long
tradition of skilled oratory. (Two such examples are
annotated below.) Given that early teachers of the deaf
most often had training as clergy, the attention to public speaking styles is not surprising. ASL oratory is
marked by its rate of delivery (slower than ordinary
conversation), the size of individual signs and signing
space (expanded from ordinary conversation, no
doubt in part because of the relatively greater distance
between signer and audience), and the incorporation
of formal, and occasionally archaic forms into the rhetorical style of the signer.

Examples of oratorical rhetoric can be found today
in religious institutions, formal occasions such as after
dinner speeches, conference keynote addresses, and
graduation addresses. For the individual hearing guest
at a deaf social event, or the few hearing participants
attending an occasion like the National Association of
the Deaf's convention, oratory can be seen live.

Sign language students will largely rely on their instructor's ability to secure examples on videotape, or to
recreate the circumstances of oratorical performance
by involving deaf visitors in the sign language class.
The latter circumstance requires the "suspension of
disbelief" on the part of the deaf visitor, whose language behaviors are carefully tuned to adjust for the
appropriate audience (Fischer 1980). The sign language class is an artificial environment for most forms

of oratory. Therefore, the instructor's responsibility will necessarily involve sensitive briefing of a deaf community member who may be invited to be a guest in a sign language class.

Folklore

Folklore here is meant to include all sorts of traditional language arts. Among these we find recitation of narratives which may have traditional themes and motifs, conventions for creating names in sign, visual and verbal jokes and games, and language art which depends on the form of signing for its aesthetic. Lentz (1980) gives a brief taxonomy of folklore genres which include some of the most important story types, motifs, and joke formulae.

Storytelling — narrative — is perhaps the most obvious and easiest to incorporate into a sign language classroom. While I do not refer here to retelling of children's stories from Western literature (e.g., Little Red Riding Hood, but see below for "literature in translation"), I do recognize that retelling experiences from childhood has value for both the storyteller and the audience. Hearing students can always deepen their appreciation of the special life circumstances of deaf people. The deaf signers we call on (or view on videotape) often share the experiences of residential school life, separation from home at an early age whether that separation is physical or psychological. Certainly deaf signers share the awakening of the realization that their deafness separates them from some of their human companions and brings them closer to others. Stories abound which encapsulate the deaf community's view of the World as hostile or mysterious, in contrast

to signing and the Deaf domain as familiar and know-
able. What new stories will come out of the more recent
experiences of deaf adults who have been "mainstreamed" and how the received wisdom may change
as the conditions of deafness-as-isolation change from
isolation of the group (residential school) to isolation of
the individual (mainstreamed school) cannot be easily
predicted.

ABC stories (also called alphabet stories or A–to–Z
stories) are one of the most complex and at the same
time compact verbal art forms in ASL. An ABC story
gives a quick narrative, but is highly constrained in its
structure. It is composed on only 26 signs, each using
the handshapes of the one-handed manual alphabet in
order. (A subtype of the ABC story might be called the
1–2–3 story, in which handshapes for numbers constitute the formal constraining principle.) Traditional
themes include potentially taboo topics such as sex,
ghost stories, or tales that mock religion. ABC stories
may be frozen, memorized static artifacts of the culture, or in the hands of a few skilled signers may be a
productive art form created on the spot, tailored to particular themes, and given fresh life.

A simple demonstration of the variation in skill at
manipulating ABC stories comes from asking signers if
they know any ABC stories. Some people will not admit knowing what the idea is, until the questioner
quote the first 3–4 signs of a traditional ABC story. The
signer whose performance skills do not include productive creation of stories within this form may then be
moved to either show the memorized form, or reveal
that indeed he or she only knows the first half dozen
signs of that story. The rare person who has the ability

to create or recreate ABC stories will then display his or her skills. Sign language students, after being exposed to one or more examples of ABC stories (either live or on videotape), can be asked to create their own for homework.

From humor as well as narrative, the stock of traditional characters and practical jokes becomes familiar. Just as English speakers know from the few words "did you hear the one about the traveling salesman?" that a joke follows, so the ASL variant of "little moron" jokes can also be recognized. Other humor depends on visual similarity between two distinct signs (near puns). The last two chapters of Klima and Bellugi's *Signs of Language* (1979) examine in some detail the notions of poetry and wit in ASL. The exposure of sign language students to ASL humor suits Chapin's third purpose of language study, sensitizing them to a new aesthetic expression.

Performance Art

By performance art, we can include poetry (especially that composed in ASL) and other rehearsed or scripted works. Jim Cohn (1986) supports the notion of an emerging consciousness around indigenous poetic forms in ASL. He argues that images and iconic elements will make ASL poetry most translatable into spoken language. While I may disagree with his notion that true ASL poetry never existed before Alan Ginsburg's 1984 conversations at NTID (Rochester, NY) with Robert Panara, the program Cohn outlines for nurturing deaf poetry through community recognition, experimentation, and discussion is a valuable model to recreate elsewhere.

Bernard Bragg and Eugene Bergman's English (bare-bones) script of *Tales from a Clubroom* permits us distant from the performances of that play to appreciate its characters and themes. Some of the language choices are lost without a videotape of an actual performance, since the English version cannot capture the particulars of the ASL forms. *Sign Me Alice* by Gil Eastman is another script which uses a gloss transcription system to represent the signs used on stage. The story is known to hearing readers as George Bernard Shaw's *Pygmalion*, but it has been reworked to tell the conflict between the "war of the methods" in deaf education (signing vs. speech, and if signing, which variety).

Beyond ASL genres

At least two additional sources of external literary tradition inform the study of deaf sign language and its culture and community in this country. These sources include literature in translation and images of deaf people in literature, film and television. The former includes material translated from English or other languages, but performed in ASL for deaf (and general) audiences. The latter includes views of deafness and deaf people available to general audiences, both deaf and hearing, which have influenced students' stereotypes or attitudes toward hearing impairment before their entry into college level sign language instruction.

Literature in Translation

We certainly must acknowledge the importance of material translated from English or other languages in looking at the performances of National Theatre of the Deaf and other regional or college performing groups.

For example, Little Theater of the Deaf, NTD's performing ensemble for school-age audiences, often uses haiku translated from the Japanese as a featured section of its revues. The use of haiku (in English translation) has been adopted by college theater groups as a training technique. The original Japanese form of haiku, with its three line format with precise number of syllables per line (five-seven-five) and the invocation of seasonal imagery, is often followed in English translations, but is less emphasized in ASL translation, where the notion of "syllable" has no direct equivalent. Rather, the ASL version of haiku highlights building a single image with a high value on economy of signs employed to produce the mood and scene. The introduction of haiku forms has also been used as an instructional technique with grammar school-age children, who are first shown ASL translations, invited to invent their own, and helped to translate the signed versions to an English form.[2]

Haiku, then, takes on a special meaning when used with ASL translations or original forms. Ask sign language students to examine either videotaped examples or live performances, and later to create their own ASL haikus. This exercise can develop the students' appreciation for the capability of ASL to pack several semantic notions into a single sign, and for the effects of rhythm, repetition of movement, physical placement of signs in the signing space, and signer's affect in developing an aesthetically pleasing and appropriate translation.

---

[2] Dennis Cokely, personal communication.

The growing popularity of interpreted performances — that is, theatrical or musical productions with sign language interpreters involved in the performance — likewise points to a measure of acceptance among the Deaf community of participation in mainstream literary traditions. And yet, careful examination of the ways in which these translations are created and the resultant linguistic objects and their performances give us further evidence for independent aesthetic judgments which are made by the translation supervisors, directors, and performers.[3]

Literature about Deafness & Deaf People

If the schedule permits and the instructor can integrate the material, we can extend the curriculum to include consideration of deafness and deaf people in English language literature (including film). [4] Joanne Greenberg's *In this Sign* (made into a television film "Love is Never Silent") imparts a great deal of cultural information about deafness in a well-written, if somewhat sentimental, novel. Her short story "And Sarah Laughed" shows some of the same characters from an earlier time. Carson McCullers' *The Heart is a Lonely Hunter* has been recognized as a classic of literature from the American South, and portrays two quite different deaf characters in relation to the hearing world. *Children of a Lesser God*, which won awards on Broadway and in Hollywood, is available in script form and as a film, if not a live performance, gives the view of the well-meaning hearing teacher in contact with the maturing

---

[3] See Frishberg 1986 for a fuller treatment of interpreting, especially interpreting performances.

[4] For comparison, see Basso 1974.

deaf woman. It is a love story with a political and educational impact. (The differences between the original play and the adaptation to screen are instructive as well.)

Robert Panara's article (1972) about deaf characters in English language literature highlights certain stereotypes which students probably bring to their sign language classes, but which are hard to draw to the surface. Panara reveals variety of communication techniques these characters employ, and notes the heavy emphasis on sensational and exaggerated accomplishments in lipreading, speaking and the like. He also exposes the high proportion of charlatan deaf characters, those posing as deaf, but who are later revealed to have used the device for trickery.

Batson and Bergman (1985) have collected writings about and by deaf people in an anthology which may still be in print. In the first section are excerpts from the perspective of the deaf as seen by others (e.g. Turgenev, Dickens, Ambrose Bierce, Isak Dinesen), while in the second are pieces showing the deaf as seen by themselves (Albert Ballin, Julius Wiggins, Grace McGreevy).

Inserting Literature in the ASL class curriculum

In order to build and expand students' views of what constitutes literary achievement in a language without written literary form, two types of activities may be employed. First, the extensive use of film and videotaped materials can expose students to a variety of forms of literary output. These materials also engage students' attention to details of the production of signing, with the potential for repetition of identical performance by replaying particular segments of a film or tape.

What materials shall be employed? Materials used in sign language instruction might be historical films, documentaries about deafness or deaf people which include relevant samples of literary production, pedagogical materials aimed at a deaf or signing audience, or theatrical productions.

With care, an instructor may adapt materials intended for interpreter training to sign language classes at a more elementary level. Naturally, each film or videotape must be examined to determine its appropriate use with the target audience.

Where can these materials be obtained? Several organizations have tapes available for purchase or loan. Others rent to educational institutions for low cost. The Gallaudet University (Washington, D.C.) Media Distribution office updates its catalogue periodically and makes its films and videotapes available to nonprofit educational institutions. It may also make the materials available through one of the extension offices in other regions. The National Association of the Deaf (Silver Spring, MD) has in the past sold or rented video materials through its bookshop. TJ Publishers (Silver Spring, MD) has recently sent out its catalog of videotaped materials available for purchase. Included are children's stories, tapes to accompany instructional textbooks, scholarly lectures from recent conferences, and tapes modeling family communication with deaf and hearing family members. Modern Talking Picture Service (St. Petersburg, FL) offers free loan of educational captioned films and videotapes to classes with at least one deaf or hearing impaired student. Their catalogue requires careful screening, since many of the materials are simply captioned versions of general interest films and videotapes. Only some of the items have sign language or deaf content.

In addition, local public libraries, schools for the deaf, and nearby colleges or universities with larger programs serving deaf and hearing impaired students may have media collections to be shared with the regional community. Most institutions of higher education provide a budget for rental of alternative media for classroom use, and each institution's media office will have catalogues and helpful personnel to assist instructors in securing appropriate materials economically.

Films & Videotapes. Below are listed only a few samples of appropriate film and videotape materials that can be used with sign language classes to augment and support the study of literature in ASL. Instructors need to preview materials before showing them to classes for several reasons. First, the instructor needs to be certain that the chosen film or tape suits the level and purposes of the course. Next, the instructor should be certain that he or she understands each part of the material; in the case of the historical films of ASL, even experienced signers will require repeat viewing to catch all the archaic forms. Further the instructor must prepare activities for the class to focus their attention. Sometimes, more than one viewing of a film or tape is necessary for the students to be able to see the features of the material which the instructor finds pedagogically important to that level of sign language instruction. For example, some instructors will choose to show the NAD performances first with the sound on to give stu-

dents the overall sense of the performance, and later
without sound to encourage attentive viewing of particular theatrical or poetic ASL forms, without audio
distraction.[5]

The choice of whether to discuss the film or video
material using speech or sign in class depends on the
level of the class and the way in which the course is designed. To compare with spoken language instruction,
some foreign language courses require the use of target
language for all class activities. Other such courses
make a distinction between conversation instruction,
and discussion of grammar, literature and culture of
the target language, such that the former activities are
all conducted in the target language while the latter activities may use students' ordinary classroom language, especially at the lower levels of instruction.

Wherever possible, making the visual materials
available to students for repeat viewing in a language
lab or media center can prove helpful. This way the instructor may model during class the desired sort of
analysis or preferred viewing techniques, but can then
make the "reading of literature" part of the homework
activity.

Conclusion

ASL has been excluded from fulfilling foreign or second language requirements in some institutions because of claims that it has no grammar, cultural
context, or tradition of literature. The preceding remarks refute the last of these claims (while other arti-

---

[5] Karl Heider (1976) discusses preparation for using films
in classes.

cles in this issue address the first two). We have seen that a literary aesthetic can be defined prior to a written literary tradition, as in the case of Greek and Balkan epic poetry. We know that other languages which are socially stigmatized nonetheless adapt literature through translation and develop their own literary institutions. Non-Western cultures without writing traditions convey their traditions of history and philosophy within community-defined forms of expression. And, finally, the presence or absence of writing (systematized orthography) has little relationship to the existence of a traditional verbal art form.

We have discussed three genres of ASL language arts: oratory, folklore, and performance art. For each of these, examples have been offered both in explanation and in video or film for use in college-level classes. It is incumbent on the instructor to find appropriate ways to insert such examples into the curriculum and to train students to see the relevant features of these examples. In addition, literature in translation (whether performed by deaf artists or hearing artists with interpreters) can be useful to demonstrate the incorporation of culturally-valued features into the form of expression.

Appendix: Relevant Examples

American Sign Language: a student text — Baker & Cokely (1980)

The series of videotapes geared to the three student textbooks includes not only demonstration of the dialogues for each unit, but also "provides several ASL stories, poems, and dramatic prose of varying lengths and difficulty for use in the classroom or language lab." (Baker & Cokely, 1980:vii)

My Third Eye — National Theater of the Deaf (1973)

One of several early documentaries of NAD productions, this one features a variety of popular performance pieces, including personal reminiscences from deaf members of the cast, poetry, playful sign etymologies, and a fantasy about deaf views of the strange practices in the "Land of A-Ba-Ba" (among hearing people).

Preservation of Sign Language — George Veditz (1913) — NAD

An early President of the National Association of the Deaf, Veditz here gives an impassioned plea for the preservation of sign language traditions through documentation on film as well as by sign language use in schools and other institutions. The structure of his argument and his style of delivery are as worthy of attention as his message.

Memories of Old Hartford — John Hotchkiss (1913) — NAD

A reminiscence of early days at the American School for the Deaf in Hartford, Connecticut, this film and others of its era make visible the facts that (i) sign language has been recorded and preserved from nearly as early as Edison's records of spoken language, (ii) historical changes in signs and their pronunciations can be documented through such records. Hotchkiss recalls his own encounters with Laurent Clerc, David Bartlett and other early figures at ASD.

The World According to Pat: Reflections of Residential School Days — Sign Media (1986)

Pat Graybill, one of a number of accomplished alumni from the earlier days of National Theater of the Deaf, still a professional performer and more recently a college level educator, has made a videotape which "reveals the foundations of Deaf culture." (*Sign Language Studies* 54: 91-92) His portrayals of the roles that the hearing and deaf adults around children in a residential school for the deaf take on give insight into the school as a powerful binding force in deaf lives. These roles may be both the external labels "teacher" or "houseparent," as well as the traits the people assume in the functions "loving," "cruel," "authoritarian," or "well-intentioned." With cameo appearances by other deaf actors, the videotape presents the physical and psychic space familiar to many deaf viewers, and now available to sign language classes.

See What I Say — Filmaker's Library (1981)

Available as a 24-minute film or videotape, this production documents the work of Holly Near, a feminist folksinger, and Susan Freundlich, a professional performance interpreter who toured with her for several years. Their close working relationship was achieved through careful rehearsal and discussion process, which we see parts of and hear the two of them reflect on. The response of the target audience is shared through the stories of four women who have experienced the change from isolation of deaf people to more open acceptance of sign language, interpreting and performance.

Shadowing — Stage Hands, Inc. (c.1980)

This tape describes the process used by the Stage Hands, Inc., group in conjunction with the Alliance Theatre Company/ Atlanta Children's Theatre to pre-

pare and produce interpreted productions for deaf and
hearing impaired audiences. Among the areas of attention are script analysis and translation, blocking and
direction, focus (of interpreter's attention), lighting,
pre-teaching activities and reactions of theater staff/
actors to audience and interpreters. Role for hearing
impaired coach or consultant is touched on. Tape provides a good starting point for comparison with practices of interpreters in other regions of the country
and/or where the audience may not be limited to
school groups.

References

(unsigned). 1986. Brief notice of videotape viewed: The
    World According to Pat: Reflections of Residential
    School Days, by Pat Graybill (ASLRTC Tapes, pro-
    duced by Sign Media, Inc.). Silver Spring, MD: TJ
    Publishers.Sign Language Studies 54, 91-92.

Baker, Charlotte & Dennis Cokely. 1980*American Sign
    Language: a teacher's resource text on grammar and cul-
    ture*. Silver Spring, MD:TJ Publishers (with accom-
    panying videotapes)

Basso, Keith. 1974. *Portraits of "the Whiteman": Linguis-
    tic play and cultural symbols among the Western
    Apache*. Cambridge University Press.

Batson, Trent and Eugene Bergman. 1985. *Angels and
    Outcasts: An Anthology of Deaf Characters in Litera-
    ture*. Washington, D.C.: Gallaudet University Press.

Bragg, Bernard and Eugene Bergman. 1981. *Tales from
    a Clubroom*. Washington, D.C.: Gallaudet College
    Press.

Cohn, Jim. 1986. The New Deaf Poetics: Visible Poetry. *Sign Language Studies*, 52, 263-277.

Eastman, Gil. 1974. *Sign Me Alice*. Washington, D.C.: Gallaudet College Press.

Frishberg, N. 1986.*Interpreting: An Introduction*. Silver Spring, MD: RID.

Gittleman, Sol. 1978. *From Shtetl to Suburbia: the family in Jewish literary imagination*. Boston: Beacon Press.

Greenberg, Joanne. 1970. *In this Sign*. New York: Holt, Rinehart & Winston.

Greenberg, Joanne. 1973. And Sarah Laughed. In *Rites of Passage*. New York: Avon Books.

Heider, K. G. 1976. *Ethnographic Film*. Austin: University of Texas Press.

Klima, E. S. & U. Bellugi. 1979. *Signs of Language*. Cambridge, MA: Harvard University Press. (See especially Chapters 13 "Wit and Play on Signs" and 14 "Poetry and Song in a Language without Sound")

Lentz, Ella Mae. 1980. Creative Styles in American Sign Language. Paper presented at NSSLRT, Boston, October 26–30.

Lord, Albert B. 1964. *The Singer of Tales*. Cambridge, MA: Harvard University Press.

McCullers, Carson. 1967. *The Heart is a Lonely Hunter*. Boston: Houghton Mifflin Co.

Meadow, Kay. 1972. Sociolinguistics, Sign Language and the Deaf Sub-Culture. In *Psycholinguistics and Total Communication: the State of the Art*, Ed. by T.J.

O'Rourke. Washington, D.C.: American Annals of the Deaf, pp. 19-33.

Medoff, M. 1980. *Children of a Lesser God*. Clifton, NJ: J. J. White.

Panara, Robert F. 1970. The Deaf Writer in America from Colonial Times to 1970. *American Annals of the Deaf*, Part 1, 509 –512; Part 2, 673—679.

Panara, Robert F. 1972. Deaf Characters in Fiction and Drama. *The Deaf American* (May).

Scribner, Sylvia & Michael Cole. 1981. *The Psychology of Literacy*. Cambridge, MA: Harvard University Press.

Singer, Isaac Bashevis. 1978. *Nobel Lecture*. New York: Farrar Straus Giroux.

Stokoe, William, Casterline, D.C. & Croneberg, C.G. 1965. *A Dictionary of American Sign Language on Linguistic Principles*. Washington, D.C.: Gallaudet College Press. (Reprinted 1980, Linstok Press: Silver Spring, MD)

Sutton, Valerie. 1982. *Sign Writing for Everyday Use*. Newport Beach, CA: Center for Sutton Movement Writing.

Varley, John. 1978. The Persistence of Vision. In *The Persistence of Vision*. New York, NY: Dial Press. Pp. 227-272.

Witherspoon, Gary. 1977. *Language and Art in the Navajo Universe*. Ann Arbor: University of Michigan Press.

Signing Naturally: Notes on the Development of the ASL Curriculum Project at Vista College

Cheri Smith
Vista College

This chapter outlines the procedures used to identify, analyze, and organize components of an American Sign Language (ASL) curriculum. This curriculum encourages students to develop communicative competence and cultural awareness in a classroom environment that allows for natural language learning.

Why did you decide to write an ASL curriculum?

We had several reasons. In recent years there has been an increased demand for instruction in American Sign Language. It has been estimated that in California alone over 10,000 students enroll in sign language courses each year.

We knew that this increased demand was a mixed blessing. While ASL is well over 200 years old and is America's fourth most commonly used language, it has only recently been widely taught in schools and colleges. As a result, there is a dearth of instructional materials. New linguistic research has yet to be analyzed for its applications to teaching ASL in the classroom.

ASL programs often select teachers for their language fluency rather than their background in language teaching. These teachers, in turn, base their classes on student textbooks or try to develop their own instructional materials. There is no overall curricular idea which can help teachers (1) establish a cultural context for language instruction, (2) make decisions about how to sequence course materials, and (3) develop activities which allow students to progress from one-word responses to spontaneous expression of thoughts and feelings on a discourse level.

At Vista, we experienced all these problems, and tried to overcome them by developing instruction materials as needed. In 1978, we received funds to develop a legal interpreting guide. In 1980, we developed a guide to medical interpreting, focusing on pregnancy. In 1981, we developed ASL course syllabi for beginning and intermediate levels. In 1982, we developed videotapes for teaching classifiers. In 1983, we developed a series of interactive videotapes to be used in the language lab. After field testing these materials, we realized we were on the right track but knew that the materials alone were not enough.

What was missing?

The syllabi were not comprehensive enough. They were based on what individual instructors had done in class. There was not an overall structure, or a sequenced plan governing why, when, and how to introduce concepts. There were not enough supporting activities and materials to help teachers implement the syllabi. When we assessed student performance, we found that they seemed to use the grammar structures correctly yet were not able to converse naturally. Moreover, very little attention had been given to cross-cultural interactions. We needed a curriculum that addressed these issues and mapped out a two-year course of study that would help students develop proficient use of the language. We needed to teach proficiency in cross-cultural communication between deaf and hearing people.

How did you get started?

That was tough. We did not have the expertise. None of us had designed a curriculum before. We were not familiar with current research in the field.

We wrote to different ASL programs around the country and found that others, like us, had individual course outlines and materials, but nothing comprehensive or compiled in a form accessible to other ASL instructors. Most programs based their curriculum on two or three existing ASL textbooks.

The books are excellent as far as they go. One is organized according to grammatical points. From our experience, this is not the most effective way of designing a language course. Even though students master grammatical structures, they do not learn natural conversational skills. The other book is organized according to culturally relevant topics accompanied by supplemental grammar points. This text was a giant step forward because it dealt with language on a discourse level using videotapes of native signers in actual conversations. However, because the tapes were a "slice of life," they sometimes incorporated complex grammar

and advanced vocabulary and there was often a gap
between what was expressed on the tape and what students could comprehend. As a result, teachers could
not use the text and tapes to organize and sequence lessons and systematically introduce topics and expand
vocabulary.

The problem with both texts is that they do not provide a natural basis for language learning. Children do
not learn subject–verb agreement, then pronoun reference, and then subjunctive. They learn language in a
social context, in the target language, building their vocabulary on the basis of the here and now. They learn
concrete words before abstract ones. They learn by interacting with a person who introduces new words
and patterns, showing how to convey something in a
particular situation for a particular purpose.

We wrote a proposal to FIPSE (U.S. Department of
Education, Funds for Improvement of Postsecondary
Education) for three-year funding to develop the first
standardized ASL curriculum. This would provide the
means for articulation among ASL programs around
the country, and provide the basis for uniform training
and certification programs. We said we needed $90,000
a year for three years. This would pay for part-time
support for Ella Mae Lentz, Kenneth Mikos, and myself; for our editor and production coordinator, Lisa
Cahn; for our language analysts, Ben Bahan, Marlon
Kuntze, and Jamie Tucker; and our consultants, Dennis
Cokely, Carol Padden, and Peter Shaw.

FIPSE, much to our delight, gave us what we asked
for. We set our attention on figuring out how to do
background research, design a theoretically sound curricular plan, write lesson plans showing the teacher

what to teach, develop activities and aids which would not only help the teacher introduce vocabulary and grammar, but do so in a sequence and context which reflected and respected Deaf culture, identify relevant cross-cultural situations, field test the units, and disseminate the final curriculum package.

How did you orient yourselves?

We surveyed the professional and research literature, as well as textbooks, ESL curricula, and the California State guidelines for foreign language instruction. We surveyed sign language students, asking them to describe how they used ASL and assessing if their courses had prepared them to use ASL in real-life situations. We surveyed members of the Deaf community asking them to identify situations and discussion topics which frequently occurred with hearing signers.

From all of this we learned that we could not use a strictly grammar-based organization because it would teach students how to use language principles but not why or when to use them. We could not use a strictly transactional organization, teaching students what to say in typical situations (e.g., at the bank or talking to a mechanic) because such situations are neither typical nor realistic. Deaf and hearing people mainly interact in social situations. We needed an orientation that emphasized interpersonal communication.

We concluded that the "functional-notional" approach would be the most useful way to accomplish this. As Finocchiaro (1983) explains:

> [A] functional-notional approach concentrates on the purposes for which language is used. Any act of speech is functionally organized (that is, it is an

> attempt to *do* something) for a particular situation
> in relation to a particular topic.... A functional-no-
> tional approach to language learning places ma-
> jor emphasis on the *communicative purpose(s)* of a
> speech act. It focuses on what people want to do
> or what they want to accomplish through speech.
> Do they want to introduce people to each other?
> Do they want to invite someone to their home?
> Do they want to direct someone to do or not to do
> something? Do they want to talk about a picture,
> a book, a film, or something in the room they are
> in? Do they want to give sway to their creative
> impulses and recite a poem?

This was compatible with deaf-hearing social encounters. A functional-notional curriculum could help
students achieve communicative competency. Vocabulary, grammatical structures, and expressions taught
would be determined by the function. Situations which
predicted everyday deaf-hearing activities and encounters would be used to contextualize and give
meaning to the function. The indirect benefit of these
situations for students would be cultural awareness
and cross-cultural adjustment skills.

How did you actually develop the curriculum?

We designed a nine-step process. First, from the five
broad categories of functions, we identified those important in cross-cultural, deaf-hearing encounters.
(The functions listed in the 'personal' category enable
us to express emotions and feelings; 'interpersonal'
functions enable us to establish and maintain social relationships; with 'directive' functions we make requests or suggestions, persuade or convince;
'referential' functions enable us to tell about the

present, past future; 'imaginative' functions enable us to use language creatively.) We began to **select functions** most appropriate for each language level. For example:

Level 1: Exchanging personal information
          Identifying others
          Making a request

Level 2: Giving directions
          Telling what happened
          Making plans

Level 3: Complaining about health problems
          Giving instructions
          Complaining and giving advice

Level 4: Making analogies to explain something
          Persuading others
          Logical necessity

Second, we **collected language samples** by videotaping native signers engaging in dialogues. We described situations and gave each signer a specific language function to perform, using cues such as:

> You enter a restaurant and notice your friend talking with a person you don't know. You approach them to say hello.

> You want to borrow some books on a specific subject from your friend's library.

> Your friend will ask permission to borrow some-
> thing precious to you. Your friend is not good
> about returning things.

> There is a new executive director of DCARA. You
> want to know who he is, so you approach Signer
> B to ask.

The resulting dialogues helped us determine linguistic expressions native signers use with particular
functions. We then scripted dialogues for the curriculum based on this natural speech. This helped us avoid
artificial language in the curriculum.

To structure narratives, we videotaped native signers talking about family history, telling jokes, anec-
dotes, and school-day stories, giving instructions,
defining terms, relating the latest Deaf community
news and current events. In addition to helping us define expressions that co-occur with functions, this also
helped us develop narrative activities, identify vocabulary, and analyze examples of role shift.

We also invited over 25 couples to join us for pizza
and group conversation. Some did not know each other; others were related; some brought children. We
filmed the event to see the functions that occurred, the
topics people talked about, how people took turns
speaking, how they got attention, and how they lis-
tened.

Third, we filmed deaf and hearing interactions in
similar situations. We observed how communication
variables changed. By contrasting the deaf-deaf with
deaf-hearing dialogues, we began to understand the
interaction between language and culture. For example, hearing and deaf persons' approaches to identifying a third person were quite different. Deaf persons

described physical attributes, personal habits, behavior patterns, or relationships in the Deaf community. Hearing persons initially relied on more "neutral" reference points — occupation or place of residence. Because Deaf people belong to a smaller, more cohesive community, there is cultural license for familiarity and an active and cooperative search for common conversational ground.

Fourth, our analyses of these situations allowed us to identify how deaf and hearing persons organized information differently, and to understand the detailed structure of **speech acts** — how subjects are broached; what kind of information is expected; how corrections are made; how signals are given to indicate that a conversation is ending.

We were able to identify **conversational strategies** — how a person clarified points, corrected misunderstandings, rejoined, interrupted, digressed, returned to the central point, changed the subject, and so on. We also observed listening strategies — how listeners provided feedback showing understanding, empathy, surprise, and so forth, actively taking part in the conversation. Finally, we noted the errors that hearing persons most frequently made and how deaf persons adjusted.

Fifth, we took the analysis a step further and identified subtle but important **cultural differences** between the deaf and hearing worlds and analyzed how these differences affected cross-cultural communication. For example, we found that deaf and hearing persons have very different notions about success, accomplishments, embarrassment, personal space, private business, bodily functions, personal relationships, and community responsibilities.

Next, we identified a range of **topics** which were likely to be raised in conversation among deaf persons, and observed how the treatment of these topics changed in deaf-hearing interactions. Then we sequenced the topics according to language development issues, and included those of interest to students and those most germane to cross-cultural interactions. For example, Deaf people keep each other informed about the lives of others in the community. Therefore, it is essential that students learn to talk about themselves, their families, their friends, and co-workers in a consistent, familiar way with just the right amount of detail.

Seventh, we identified **situations** that hearing persons of different levels of ASL proficiency would be likely to encounter. A beginning student would probably have chance meetings and limited conversations with deaf people. Therefore, we chose situations such as bumping into someone at the bus stop, chatting with ASL teachers during a break, or talking with a deaf visitor to an ASL class. For intermediate students, who would be likely to have more extended, one-to-one interactions, we chose situations such as a party, driving with a deaf friend to a conference, or helping a deaf friend move. Advanced students may encounter the same situations, but have more complex, subtle interactions. They most likely have deaf friends and have to be able to follow complicated turns in group discussions. They would be expected to use language appropriate to a given setting, and to respond appropriately to situations that the deaf encounter with the hearing public (e.g., when a waiter assumes that the hearing person will order for her deaf friend).

Then, we specified ASL **grammar categories** appropriate to the functions. For example, directional verbs and topic-comment structures are introduced in units on "Identifying and Locating Objects" and "Making Requests." WH-question structures are introduced in the unit "Exchanging Personal Information." Role shift structures are introduced in the units "Describing Personality Traits" and "Telling What Happened."

Finally, using what we know about language learning, language teaching and cross-cultural interactions, we mapped out all this information. Then we began to write the curriculum.

What is the structure of the curriculum?

We recognize that most ASL teachers are not trained specifically as language teachers. ASL instruction is still in its early stages and there are few resources for the teacher to turn to. Therefore, we wrote detailed lesson plans that included what to teach and how to teach it. We developed activities and materials (handouts, worksheets, transparencies, and videotapes) to help teachers successfully implement the curriculum.

We created a natural language environment by giving students situations which allow them to concentrate on the purpose rather than the mechanics of conversation. Students build vocabulary starting with what they see in their immediate environment. They progress from the concrete to the abstract. They learn grammar in the context of the situations they would be likely to encounter. Students progress from structured dialogues to spontaneous exchanges. Most important, the situations teach them something about the distinctive aspects of Deaf culture and cross-cultural interaction.

There are four levels of instruction. Each consists of fourteen units focusing on a single language function. Units are divided into five sections: Introduction, Sign Production, Extended Comprehension, Interaction, and Breakaways.

Introduction — shows the teacher how to introduce the section's grammar and vocabulary in the context of a language function while staying with the target language.

Sign Production — shows how to drill students to develop the signing characteristics that lead to fluency — accuracy, speed, cadence, intonation, emphasis, and continuity.

Extended Comprehension — provides narratives which allow students to devise comprehension strategies to discern meaning from the overall context of a situation rather than from single words and phrases. The advanced levels include lectures on culturally relevant issues.

Interaction — provides activities that are a) highly structured, e.g., cued dialogues; b) moderately structured, e.g., role playing; and c) minimally structured, e.g., situational dramas and open discussions. Culture is taught both implicitly and explicitly through handouts and role-play situations.

Breakaways — go over concepts and techniques that require continuous work. For example, we do exercises aimed at creating a language community in the classroom. We work on numbers and fingerspelling. We have students engage in activities that help them develop spatial awareness and perception of the signer's perspective. We work on facial expressions that have both grammatical and emotive significance. Then we use activities to help students learn and retain vocabulary.

If students are allowed to learn language naturally, they always develop their comprehension skills more quickly than their expressive skills. We take full advantage of this by introducing everything in the target language, in a meaningful context (i.e., a story, a dialogue, or a situation), and by providing videotapes which expose students to native signers with different signing styles. This teaches students to rely on the familiar to understand the unfamiliar.

What impact do you hope the curriculum will have?

From the feedback we have received from the eight field-test sites, as well as from Canada and England, we believe that the curriculum will substantially improve the quality of ASL instruction. We believe that students will develop conversational skills that easily transfer what they learn in class to real-life situations. The cultural behaviors and sensitivity that students learn allow them to interact in a manner that is comfortable for Deaf community members. Most important, it provides students with the tools to continue to learn the language in the community. This curriculum, along with on-going ASL linguistic research and original artistic works being produced by the Deaf community, will continue to demonstrate that ASL is the subtle, elegant, powerful language of a rich, complex culture.

References

Asher, J. J. 1982. *Learning Another Language Through Actions.* Los Gatos, CA: Sky Oaks Productions, Inc.

Brislin, R. W. 1981. *Cross-Cultural Encounters: Face-to-Face Interaction.* Elmsford, NY: Pergamon Press, Inc.

Finocchiaro, M. & C. Brumfit. 1983. *The Functional-Notional Approach: From Theory to Practice.* NY: Oxford University Press.

Gaston, J. 1984. *Cultural Awareness Teaching Techniques.* Brattleboro, VT: Pro Lingua Associates.

Krashen, S. D. 1982. *Principles and Practice in Second Language Acquisition.* Elmsford, NY: Pergamon Press, Inc.

Oller, J. W. Jr. & P. A. Richard-Amato, Eds. 1983. *Methods That Work: A Smorgasbord of Ideas for Language Teachers.* Rowley, MA: Newbury House Publishers, Inc.

Munby, J. 1978. *Communicative Syllabus Design.* Cambridge: Cambridge University Press.

Stevick, E. W. 1986. *Images and Options in the Language Classroom.* NY: Cambridge University Press.

Wilkins, D. A. 1976. *Notional Syllabuses.* Oxford: Oxford University Press.

Who is Qualified to Teach American Sign Language?

Jan Kanda and Larry Fleischer
California State University, Northridge

The field of sign language teaching is quite old, but professional recognition of American Sign Language (ASL) teaching is relatively new, spurred by the academic community's recent recognition of this form of communication — indigenous to Deaf people in the United States — as a legitimate language, grammatically distinct from English. With this recognition came federal legislation in the late 1970's mandating the provision of sign language-related services for deaf people. Since that time there has been a rapid proliferation of sign language classes offered at U.S. colleges and universities.

What makes someone qualified to teach American Sign Language? The answer will vary depending on the level of education where the individual teacher is working which may include K–12, community college, college/university, or adult education settings. However, identifiable education and knowledge, along with certain skills and attitudes, are prerequisite regardless of the setting in which ASL teachers work.

1. Sign Language teachers must respect the language and its history

Concern and discussion regarding the qualifications of sign language teachers is not a recent phenomena. Among the many responsibilities he assumed upon his arrival in America from France, Laurent Clerc considered the careful preparation of his colleagues to teach the language of signs primary. Hundreds of deaf and hearing teachers proudly said, "I am one of his disciples" (Lane, 1984). While many of those following Clerc maintained the beauty and quality of the language, concern was expressed by members of the Deaf community that the language was disintegrating in clarity, structure, and accuracy due to conditions in deaf education, negative societal attitudes, and poor sign language instruction provided to hearing people working with Deaf children and adults. Thomas Hopkins Gallaudet (1847), recognizing that ASL was unique because it had no written form, warned that "the language of signs is not to be learned from books. It must be learned, in a great degree, from the living, looking, acting model." The teacher, then, actually becomes the text book resulting in an even more critical need for truly knowledgeable, skilled, qualified teachers of sign language.

Concerned about attempts to restrict the use of signs and the emergence of "new signs", Dr. J. Schuyler Long (1918) wrote

> ...the sign language is very much a live language. It is impossible for those who do not understand it to comprehend its possibilities with the deaf, its powerful influence on the moral and social happiness of those deprived of hearing and its won-

derful power of carrying thought to intellects
which would otherwise be in perpetual darkness.

In 1913, the National Association of the Deaf (NAD)
began a project to preserve the integrity of sign language by means of film. In one of those films, George
Veditz, then president of NAD, made an impassioned
plea for the preservation of sign language, stating

> We must, with these various films, protect and
> pass on our beautiful signs as we have them now.
> As long as we have deaf people on earth, we will
> have signs and as long as we have our films, we
> can preserve our beautiful sign language in its
> original purity. It is my hope that we all will love
> and guard our beautiful sign language as the no-
> blest gift God has given to deaf people.

Outsiders, however, continued to discredit and
even harm the language which Deaf leaders such as
Clerc and Veditz tried so desperately to preserve. Early
linguists misclassified it as a nonverbal means of communication — something that had no grammatical
rules and which could not deal with abstractions or the
evolving vocabulary needs of the Deaf population. English forms of signing began to emerge, misleading
students of the language as to what the real language
was or how it functioned. In 1938, another Deaf leader,
Tom Anderson, said

> I believe that the sign language as it came to me
> through the acknowledged masters has suffered
> in the hands of people who have taken it up with-
> out proper grounding in theory and practice.
> These people whom I have observed seem to
> have little respect for the language as a noble

means of communicating noble thoughts...tend-
ing to bring forward an inferior sign language
which we refer to as *a* sign language more correctly than *the* sign language.

William C. Stokoe's work caused linguists to recon-
sider their earlier classification of sign language, and
during the past twenty years American Sign Language
has been recognized as a fully developed, rule-gov-
erned language which is used by the majority of the
Deaf community in the United States and Canada
(Baker and Cokely, 1980). This research, along with a
changing social climate, has led to a new acceptance
and respect for ASL; more and more schools are offering formal courses of instruction in sign language. In
addition, the plethora of recent state and federal legislation which has opened professional and educational
doors for Deaf people has stirred a desire to learn sign
language in an ever-widening circle of people.

American Sign Language is highly prized and increasingly valued by members of the Deaf community,
as the language of any community is cherished by its
members. Those who teach sign language must respect
and be sensitive to the historical minority status and to
the oppression of the language and those who use it.
ASL teachers must preserve the accuracy and quality
of the language they teach and must safeguard the
field of ASL instruction — preventing, even fighting
against, those unqualified people who attempt to teach
something in which they have limited skill, limited
knowledge of its history and little respect for its value
to members of the Deaf community.

2. Sign Language teachers should feel comfortable interacting within the Deaf community — demonstrating their fluency in ASL, as well as their knowledge of and comfort with the culture.

By definition, a second language teacher is one who helps another person learn a language which is not his or her native language (Alatis *et al.*, 1981). Effective second language instruction focuses on the culture in which the second language is used as well as the language. This means that those who teach a language and culture must display communicative and cultural competence. They must be able to interact in a variety of settings with a variety of individuals — using the language and following the social norms appropriate for each of those different settings.

Instructors of ASL should demonstrate above-average ability in the use of the language and in the ability to interact comfortably with individuals who adhere to Deaf cultural norms and values and who use ASL as their primary mode of communication. There should be a "gut-level" sense for the language — not just the intellectual grasp of rules and principles one obtains from reading the research, attending ASL classes, or completing a teacher preparation program. There should be a sense for when and where the "rules" can be broken, where the language is used in a poetic sense versus a literal sense, how humor is used in the language, the variety and characteristics of registers, and the rules for shifting registers. In addition, ASL teachers should have strong, positive attitudes and feelings in support of the language — along the lines of those shown by Thomas H. Gallaudet, George Veditz, and Tom Anderson.

These competencies come only with time — using the language and interacting with Deaf people who are fluent in the use of ASL in a variety of settings. Sign Language teachers should interact with and relate to the members of the Deaf community — to maintain contact with and respect for the world view and shared experiences of this group as they are expressed in the shared language of the community. Only in this way can teachers stay current with the living, evolving language of ASL and demonstrate sensitivity for and identify with those who use the language. When teachers maintain this kind of contact and involvement, the Deaf community gains a greater sense of trust for the quality of teaching provided by the teacher and for the program in which s/he works.

3. Sign Language teachers must be good teachers. They should have completed formal study of the language and of educational and pedagogical principles.

The field of sign language teaching is quite old, but professional recognition of American Sign Language (ASL) teaching is relatively new. In the past fifteen years there has been a rapid proliferation of sign language classes offered at U.S. colleges and universities. In fact, approximately 3200 people teach sign language at 800 such institutions; however, none of these teachers hold a graduate degree in ASL teaching (Baker-Shenk, 1987). In fact, very few have received any kind of formal academic training directly relevant to their work as teachers. The majority do hold undergraduate degrees, but these are in fields not related to sign language, interpreting, or second language teaching.

As the status of sign language teachers moves closer to that of foreign language teachers in high schools and colleges, the advanced preparation of ASL teachers in the 21st century is inevitable; educational preparation and teacher certification will become a common expectation of anyone who wishes to become an ASL instructor. Great strides are being made in this direction and are undergirded by such projects as the Western Maryland College graduate program for teachers of sign language where students receive rigorous preparation based on educationally proven tenets of instruction, linguistic research, and proven components of Deaf culture.

Like teachers of French, Latin, or Japanese, ASL teachers should demonstrate that they have studied the language they teach — completing courses in grammar and structure, literature, and translation in addition to whatever formal education is required of teachers at the particular level of education in which the individual wishes to teach. A theoretical base in pedagogical principles appropriate to the age of the target student population is mandatory, as well as an educational base in educational foundations, educational philosophy, integration of affective, cognitive, and psychomotor domains, metacognition, learning styles, and whole brain instruction.

Table 1 outlines minimal educational requirements, as well as suggested certification, and other characteristics of qualified teachers at each instructional level.

Table 1. Qualifications for Teaching ASL

	High School	College and University	Community and Adult Education
Education	Bachelors in ASL/Deaf Studies or related field	Bachelors in ASL/Deaf Studies or related field. Master's/doctorate in ASL, linguistics, Deaf Studies, or Education	Bilingual Workshops/courses in adult education curricula, testing, linguistics of ASL, second language instruction. Min. high school diploma, prefer bachelors degree
Certification	State teaching certificate in foreign language or social studies	S.I.G.N.[a]	State certificate in adult and/or community education
Fluency	Should have bilingual competency that has been tested by S.I.G.N., state credentialing examination, or other competent body of examiners		
Interaction with Deaf Community	Should be able to effectively interact with adult members of the Deaf community, displaying cultural competency; should display strong positive attitudes of respect for the language, culture, and community; "attitudinal deafness"		
Other	Demonstrated competence in teaching	Min. 5 years teaching experience. Engage in research of ASL, instruction techniques, language acquisition, etc. Be published in the field	Demonstrated competence in teaching

[a] Sign Instructors Guidance Network (please note that S.I.G.N. recently changed their name to Association of American Sign Language Teachers (AASLT))

4. Sign language teachers should be familiar with second language teaching theory and methodology.

As more research is available on ASL and its complexities are revealed, current instructional practices of sign language programs are being re-examined and, in many cases, reoriented and reshaped to enhance the teaching of ASL parallel to the teaching of a foreign or modern language. In fact, a study of the literature on successful second language instruction and successful ASL classes will reveal an obvious, but often overlooked, fact: there is no difference. After all, what is successful second language instruction? It is "any activity on the part of one person intended to facilitate the learning by another person of a language which is not his or her native one" (Modern Language Association, 1961). Having command of a vast store of knowledge does not make one competent in teaching; one must be able to effectively convey the information to students in order to be a qualified teacher of ASL.

In the spring of 1961, a team of five foreign language teachers and specialists, under the auspices of the Modern Language Association of America, studied the quality of language teaching throughout the United States by observing 1,011 classes taught by 747 different teachers. The characteristics reported in 1961 are still valid today in reflecting the essence of good language instruction whether the language involved is spoken or signed.

> We conclude by listing the nine features that characterized most of the successful classes we observed:

(1) The class is at ease in working with the foreign language, and seldom reverts to the native language to express an idea.

(2) Interest is high and students come to class with a real desire to learn by participating.

(3) Neither teacher nor student depends on the book. Materials fit the interests and abilities of the students and follow the principles of sound foreign language teaching. Because their cultural content is significant and accurate, they are not stereotyped.

(4) The students do most of the speaking. The teacher gives the setting for discussion, asks key questions to direct it, gives cues in case of difficulty, and gradually subordinates his own participation.

(5) Control of the class is with the teacher at all times. The students look to him for direction and timing. They are made aware of the objectives of the foreign language learning and of how a technique or exercise will help them learn.

(6) Standards of performance are high. The teacher sees that students are neither over- nor under-challenged, and tests are designed to appraise what has been learned.

(7) A variable, or unusual, seating arrangement often indicates that the teacher will be interesting to observe and that he is probably willing to experiment.

(8) As the student enters the classroom the atmosphere encourages him to use the foreign language and to assume his foreign role.

Throughout the learning process the teacher creates situations (or leads students to create them) which lead to appreciation and understanding of the foreign culture.

(9) The teacher's personality — demanding, yet fair and patient — leads his students to a high level of performance. His lessons are well planned, and the techniques of presentation and drill are used strategically and correctly to achieve the purpose of each type of exercise. If desired results are not attained with one technique, the teacher tries another. The teacher's manner makes students want to learn the foreign language, not just because it presents interesting problems to solve or things to say, or because it is fun, but because working under his confident and enthusiastic direction is appealing in itself.

Altman (1981) said, "Only the second language teacher can facilitate the when, where, and how of learning another language — or can single-handedly thwart it. The responsibility is awesome; the power to affect people's lives very real. It is a responsibility we choose when we make the decision to become second language teachers." It is critical that ASL teachers be properly prepared as second language instructors in order to carry out this responsibility.

5. Sign language teachers should be engaged in personal and professional growth and development.

In addition to greater formal preparation, teachers will also be expected to be leaders in the field of ASL, participating in linguistic research, publishing in major journals, and being active in professional educational and linguistic organizations. In order to do these things, ASL teachers must receive more advanced preparation; it is no longer enough just to "sign well" or to "be deaf." Teachers need to be learners — advancing their own education — learning from other ASL teachers through observation, exchange, and involvement in professional educational organizations — learning from their students and from their reflecting on their own teaching/learning experiences (Shute and Webb, 1984).

6. ASL teachers are human beings first, teachers second, and teachers of ASL third.

It is essential that we, as second language teachers, never forget the "priority of our roles in the classroom: first, to be a human being; then, to be a teacher; and only third, to be a teacher of languages" (Alatis *et al.*, 1981). The most successful teachers care about themselves and their students as human beings. This sometimes means bending the rules or crossing the barrier of professional distance in order to develop the rapport with students that allows both teacher and student to be vulnerable.

> To attempt to fulfill even a small fraction of the many role expectations they face would require the patience of Job, the strength of Tarzan, the endurance of Superman, and quite possibly the nine lives of a cat! Frankly, the reality of ordinary classroom life is sufficient to tax many teachers to the limits of their ability. (Alatis *et al.*, 1981)

We teach not because we are perfect — not because we have mastered every aspect of the language or because we have all the answers — but because we are in-

volved in the dynamic process of becoming. We need
to remember that teachers are also individuals with individual needs and individual abilities. Attention to
those needs and the development of those abilities will
result in a well-rounded, balanced ASL instructor who
can deal with the stresses of the classroom and the
challenge of keeping up with a rapidly evolving field.

Conclusion

What makes one qualified to teach ASL? Linguistic and
cultural competence undergirded by interaction with
members of the Deaf community and accompanied by
proper attitudinal characteristics are prerequisite. In
addition, an ASL teacher should be educated, demonstrating knowledge and application of educational and
pedagogical principles along with formal study of the
language being taught. Sign language teachers should
be able to integrate second language teaching theory
and methodology in their classrooms. They should be
engaged in activities leading to personal and professional growth and development. Finally, ASL teachers
should recognize they need first to be human beings;
then to be teachers, and third, to be teachers of American Sign Language.

References

Altman, H. 1981. What is second language teaching? In
    J. Alatis, H. Altman and P. Alatis (Eds.) *The Second
    Language Classroom: Directions for the 1980's*, pp 7–
    19. New York: Oxford University Press.

Anderson, T. 1938. What of the Sign Language? *American Annals of the Deaf* Vol. 83, No. 1, Jan., pp 120–130.

Baker-Shenk, C. 1987. Unpublished paper.

Baker, C. & D. Cokely. 1980. *American Sign Language, A Teacher's Guide to Grammar and Culture*. Silver Spring, MD: National Association of the Deaf, 1980.

Gallaudet, T. 1847. The Natural Language of Signs and Its Value and Uses in the Instruction of the Deaf and Dumb, *American Annals of the Deaf,* Vol I, pp 55–59; 79–93.

Lane, H. 1984.*When the Mind Hears*, pp 206–251. New York: Random House.

Long, J. 1918. *The Sign Language: A Manual of Signs* (Washington).

Modern Language Association of America. 1961. *Good Teaching Practices: A Survey of High School Foreign Language Classes*, p. 243.

Shute, W. & C. Webb. 1984. Docemur Docendo: He Who Teaches Learns, unpublished paper.

Veditz, G. 1913. The Preservation of the Sign Language, Washington, DC: National Association of the Deaf. Translation by Carol Padden.

An Introduction to the Culture of Deaf People in the United States: Content Notes & Reference Material for Teachers

Tom Humphries
San Diego Community College

Introduction

Along with the growth in interest in American Sign Language has come a growth in understanding the culture of the people from whom this language comes. Some information about the lives of Deaf people is provided either by design or by accident in ASL classes—when we teach ASL, we hardly can avoid being questioned about different aspects of Deaf people's lives, about what they think and what they do.

Students of ASL want and need this information about the people whose language they are learning. Others, who are not studying ASL, also are seeking an understanding of Deaf people beyond what they are able to observe themselves. On the one hand, there is real curiosity about the culture of Deaf people, and on the other hand, a strong skepticism that there is significant difference between Deaf people and the hearing people among whom they live.

Unfortunately, it has been observed that much of the information being given to students of ASL and others who wish to study the culture of Deaf people is sociological, psychological, or educational information—or is focused only on specific behaviors that quickly become stereotypical. It has proven difficult to get at and put into a curriculum the ideology, the designs, and the symbols and their meaning that make up the system of cultural knowledge that Deaf people pass from one generation to the next. It is therein that the understanding and difference that many are so curious about are to be found.

If we are to attain and sustain the credibility of both the culture of these people and the courses that we offer, our curriculum must be approached from a theoretical framework that helps us to interpret for the student the data that is available about Deaf people. There is, of course, plenty of data. The everyday "talk" of Deaf people, their folk tales and myths, poetry, political statements, writings in English, public performances, jokes, labels—*as well as* behaviors—are all pathways into this culture, if we have a way of interpreting them.

In a sense, cultural analysis is always incomplete.[1] But what is clear is that in studying culture we are seeking what Deaf people know and how they interpret their world.

Our role as teachers of courses in Deaf culture, then, is to help the student interpret the data that Deaf people offer us to examine. How do Deaf people organize their world and the meaning attached to it? What are

---

[1] C. Geertz, The Interpretation of Cultures. 1973. NY: Basic Books. Chap. 1.

the designs for living that Deaf people have created and follow or wish to follow? What are the beliefs that Deaf people have about themselves, their group, and others? What are the essentials that Deaf people consider necessary for a Deaf way of being? What are the underlying structures of which Deaf people's everyday actions are surface expressions? What are the ideological principles upon which the structures are based? All these and more are the questions we need to ask ourselves as we prepare to teach.

The course notes and reference materials below are an example of how a course may be organized, both to raise and begin to answer some of these questions. Some of the reference materials may not be available to some teachers. That is definitely a problem. Valuable data such as videotapes of public performances, and ASL poetry, films, published writings of Deaf authors, and even some research papers are often not for sale, not held in libraries, and not available for loan from personal collections. Still, there is data if we are serious about obtaining it. There is no doubt that various materials can be used to teach the same content; one need not be bound by the materials described below. No doubt also other topics than these could be discussed.

Required:

Padden & Humphries. *Deaf in America: Voices from a Culture*. 1988. Cambridge, MA: Harvard University Press.

Suggested student reading list (required, library reserve):

Baker, C. How does 'sim-com' fit into a bilingual approach to education. In *Proceedings National Symposium on Sign Language Research & Teaching*. 1978. Silver Spring, MD: NAD.

Bergman, E. & B. Bragg. *Tales from a Clubroom*. 1981. Washington: Gallaudet University Press. 15-18, 22-24, 36-39, 58f, 113.

Flournoy, J. et al. Selected letters from the *American Annals of the Deaf & Dumb*. 1855-1858.

Frishberg, N. Signers of tales: A case for literary status of an unwritten language, *Sign Language Studies* 59. 1988.

Gannon, J. *Deaf Heritage: A Narrative History of Deaf America*. 1987. Silver Spring, MD: NAD.

Geertz, C. *The Interpretation of Cultures*. 1973, NY: Basic Books Chap.1.

Jacobs, L. *A Deaf Adult Speaks Out*. 1974. Washington, Gallaudet University Press. Chapter 7.

Kluwin, T. The grammaticality of manual representations of English in classroom settings, *American Annals of the Deaf*, June 1981.

Mow, S. How do you dance without music? In Jacobs, 1974 and S. Wilcox, *American Deaf Culture*. Silver Spring, MD: Linstok Press, 1989.

Poems from *Manus*, literary magazine of the *Buff & Blue*, student newspaper, Gallaudet College.

Rutherford, S. Funny in deaf—not in hearing, *Journal of American Folklore* 96: 381. 1983. Reprinted in S. Wilcox, *American Deaf Culture*. Silver Spring, MD: Linstok Press, 1989.

Supalla, S. Manually coded English: The modality question in signed language development. In *Issues in Sign Language Research: Psychology*. Siple & Fischer, eds. Chicago: University of Chicago Press. 1991.

The "content notes" section following the reading list suggests topics, offers notes on each topic, and explains how the readings and other materials relate to these topics. These are nothing more than content notes; how the teacher handles each unit is very much open. Lectures, group discussions, guest speakers, role playing, debates, role reversal, case studies, and many other teaching strategies and activities are possible but not discussed here.

I. Topic: Culture & constructing cultural realities

Purpose:

1. To give the student the working definition of culture and the theoretical framework used in the course for analysis of the data to be presented.

2. To clarify what it means to study a culture and the problem of interpretation of a culture.

3. To help the student understand what it means to be of a culture, to understand that they are themselves of a culture, and that Deaf people are also of a culture.

Required reading:

Clifford Geertz. *The Interpretation of Cultures.* 1973. NY:
    Basic Books. Chapter 1.

Content notes:

In this course we will view culture as Geertz does, as
the search for meaning. Geertz describes culture as
webs of significance. To understand the culture, we
will attempt to find the core symbols around which it
is organized and the underlying structures of which
they are surface expressions; i.e. the ideological principles upon which they are based.

Also following Geertz, we will look for the designs
for living, the "mechanism" and "recipes" that constitute Deaf people's lives. What are the scripts that Deaf
people follow in their daily lives? Why do the scripts
take this particular form? On what meaning are they
based?

Geertz describes the study of culture as an interpre-
tative science in search of meaning. Culture is a context
within which behaviors, institutions, or processes are
described. Cultural analysis is guessing at meaning, assessing the guesses, and drawing explanatory conclu-
sions from the better guesses.

We must do this while keeping in mind Deaf people's normal-ness without reducing their particularity.
As we see how their interpretation of the world differs
from that of other cultural groups, we must return
again and again to the realization that creating an ideology, organizing meaning, acting out designs for living—all are *cultural* processes common to all peoples.
Deaf people engage in these processes and come up

with their own specific paradigms of meaning but they are not alone in doing this.

An important point to remember is that culture is historical, that is, culture is created over generations and transmitted to each succeeding generation. Like language, culture is particular to the people who create it. The culture of Deaf people today did not emerge a few years ago when people started talking about Deaf people's difference in terms of culture. The culture of Deaf people in the United States has evolved over many generations, going back into the 19th century, and has roots beyond that, in other Deaf cultures of Europe.

Culture is historical also in the sense that a person without exposure to a culture must create a design for living from scratch. A person with a culture is a person who has inherited a particular way of being. This is an important concept of our development as humans. Geertz says that culture is how we complete ourselves.

Since we are all cultural beings, we have our own way of interpreting the world. We attach meaning to everything we do and to what we experience. This meaning is the meaning that we have learned from our exposure to our particular culture. Other people, of other cultures, will do the same thing; only, their system of meaning used to interpret the world will be theirs and will differ in large and small ways from our own. For this reason objectivity in the analysis of another culture, and even of our own, is probably not an achievable goal. We must know that although we are seeking to know how Deaf people view themselves and their world, we are seeing and understanding through the filter of our own culture.

II. Topic: Learning to be Deaf.

Purpose: To stress the fact that culture is learned, and discover what it is that Deaf children learn.

Required reading:

Carol Padden & Tom Humphries. *Deaf in America: Voices from a Culture.* 1988. Cambridge, MA: Harvard University Press. Chapter 1.

Content notes:

It is very helpful in understanding the culture to look at children's "errors," which are not in fact really errors but clear attempts to apply what they are learning from their culture. An example (from the reading) is the conversation of a Deaf interviewer with two young Deaf sisters in a Deaf family, Vicki 5 and Helen 7. They are talking about a friend who signs.

Many Deaf people have memories of discovering "deafness." This is not what it seems on the surface. It is pretty easy to see signs of this process in children and in the memories of adults. Sam Supalla tells about discovering that the girl next door is hearing—thus he learns something about "others."

In most stories Deaf people tell about their childhood, hearing people, these "others," are all around, but they are not disruptive to the Deaf person's own family life. But as these children get older, they realize that they must learn about the minds of others. A comment (from the reading) by a Deaf man from a Deaf family helps us see this: "Would you believe, I never knew I was deaf until I first entered school."

Most people when they read or are told about this comment think that he meant that he never realized before that he could not hear sounds. This is not his meaning at all. He knew what the sign DEAF meant at home; it was used to refer to 'us,' family and friends who make up his world. Then he goes to school and finds quickly that it has a different meaning. The people in school use DEAF to mean 'not like us' and 'a remarkable (easily noted) condition.' This contrasts with his meaning of the same sign, 'one who behaves as expected.'

What this man and other Deaf children learn is that there is another theory of them, different from the one that they learned through exposure to their Deaf families. This other theory of them, held by "others," defines them as "having an affliction." In other words, Deaf children are viewed as a displacement from what is expected, and will learn that an entirely different set of assumptions are the basis of this theory "others" have about them. So we have a portrait of Deaf children learning that they are "unmarked" until they discover others' definition of them.

We can contrast these examples with the theories of the children (from the reading) who have not had exposure to the culture of Deaf people.

What emerges from these stories of both kinds, these comments by children, is that hearing or not hearing does not in itself have significance; it takes on significance in the contexts of other sets of meaning. What would happen to a child who hears in a Deaf family? What will he learn? Look at this statement (from the reading) by such a child: "I never knew I was hearing until I was six. I never suspected in any way that I was different from my parents and siblings."

He is not pretending to be deaf or blocking his hearing. He simply understands sound in a way he can reconcile with the experiences of his family. What does this tell us? That the belief that there are things that can be known directly without being interpreted by our cultures is incorrect. Very little we know is not filtered through our everyday experience.

These stories tell us that the whole idea of someone being "deaf" (afflicted) is a theory held by others, not one held by Deaf people themselves. They certainly know of this theory and some may internalize it as their own, but it is still a theory of "others." Leaning to be Deaf is not a unique process. It is a process exactly like the process other, non-Deaf children go through. Exposed to a culture, Deaf culture, children proceed to learn it. What they learn is a theory of themselves, a theory of "others," and they learn about the theory "others" have of them.

III. Topic: Images of origin

1. To discover the imagery that Deaf people use to talk about their origin.
2. To understand the basic beliefs Deaf people have about the essentials for being.

Required reading:

Carol Padden & Tom Humphries. *Deaf in America: Voices from a Culture.* 1988. Cambridge, MA: Harvard University Press. Chapter 2.

Content notes:

Most cultures have ideas about how the people of the culture came to be. So talking about origins is talking about beginning but also about *being*, about existing. What is a good example of a story of origin that you can think of off the top of your head? The Judaeo-Christian story of creation in *Genesis* is an example. The "big-bang" theory and evolution is another.

It should be clear that there is a lot of mythology involved in stories of origin. Exactly what is myth and what is truth is sometimes hard to decide, and people will disagree about myth and truth. But it is certain that with the passage of time and retelling, myths do form around truth. Many stories of origin become myth or folk tales. They are not less important or less meaningful because of this. They do tell the story of how people believe they began. These folk tales also carry an important message: they tell what is the lifeblood of the group. They can also tell what are the essentials for the people to exist and continue to exist as a people.

The Epée story (from the reading) that is told in France and the United States is one story of origin that Deaf people tell. This story has taken on the characteristics of a folk tale. It is usually told with a sense of drama and formality by the best storytellers. The story means a great deal to French Deaf people. Why is it so important to them, and apparently to American Deaf people also?

There is a lot of myth in the story. Harlan Lane in his books tells us that the Abbé de l'Epée did not encounter the two women on a dark and stormy night but instead met them on his rounds through a poor section of Paris. He didn't have a revelation of his vocation as the myth has it but instead was approached by the girls' mother, who asked him to give her daughters religious instruction.

This story is important because these people chose to tell it, and not a story of the founding of their local club or a story about some other nationally known Deaf figure like Laurent Clerc. They picked this story. It is not just about Epée. It is about the transition of Deaf people from a world in which they live alone in small isolated communities to a world in which they have a rich community and language. In this sense this is a story of origin, a folk tale that informs us about the beginning of a people and their language.

The storyteller has passed on an image: Epée going from the darkness of night into the light of the house; and this is a central image. Many folk tales choose this image of going from darkness into light in their stories of origins. In the biblical story, God proclaims that there should be light. In the big bang theory there is presumably a flash of light with the explosion. The light is the beginning.

And what does the light represent in the Epée story? The establishment of the first great community of Deaf people around the school the Abbé founded. The French Deaf writer Massieu informs us (from the reading) what it was like before the Deaf people came together in a community. Each new generation of children entering the schools established by Epée or one of his followers inherited a history, a tradition, passed down in the school and the community organized around it.

While the folk tale of Epée is a story about the creation of this community, it is also a story about how

Deaf people must find one another. Until they have been delivered to the community, they cannot learn the history of the group. At the end of Epée's wandering is the light and warmth of the house where Deaf people are. At the end of Deaf people's wandering is the succor and warmth of the community.

The Epée story is part of the American Deaf folk mythology as well as of the French. For American Deaf people also it symbolizes the transition from an undesirable to a desirable state of being. One particularly emotional example (from the reading) of invoking this image of Epée and what he represents was written by J. J. Flournoy in the 1850s:

> We are not beasts, for all our deafness! We are MEN! The Era of De l'Epée has been the epoch of our birth of mind. After a long night of wandering, our planet has at length attained an orbit around a central luminary.

American Deaf people also have other folk tales that reveal the same recognition of the importance of the community. This particular story (from the reading) began as a family story and has become more public, with wide circulation. It is the story of Joshua Davis, a young Deaf boy at the time of the Civil War. The story has the same core in all versions: a hapless Deaf boy, caught by soldiers and about to be hanged as a spy, is saved by an officer who has Deaf relatives. The boy is not saved by his gestures, nor by the speech of his parents, and probably not by fingerspelling alone, but he is saved by the special knowledge that Deaf people have, knowledge of the community. The story is called "Sign Language Saves a Life," but the story also tells us what one cannot count on to save one's life: gesture or speech. Only the special knowledge gained from other Deaf people can save one's life.

These stories affirm basic beliefs of the group. They are, in a way, instructions, which recall the past and teach about how one's life needs to be conducted; they show what must be valued. Another American variation of these instructions is seen in the "Preservation of the Sign Language" by George Veditz (from the reading). Veditz chose powerful symbols and images to guide you from the good world of Epée, where signed language is ideally integrated into the lives of Deaf people, to a bad world, where the "cruel hearted" have "snatched away" their language. When this happens they fall into despair, "chained at the ankles," and imprisoned as they watch others "free to wander at will."

A more modern example of this same theme of struggle was seen in the National Theater of the Deaf production of *My Third Eye* (from the reading). One scene has particularly brutal images and evolved from a member of the cast's experiences and dreams. In the scene a girl is forced to speak, which she cannot do to the satisfaction of an unknown power, and unable to escape, she is consigned to a terrible death by drowning.

Thus we have stark images here of hanging, imprisonment, and death by drowning. The stories warn about worlds of darkness, despair, and nonexistence. What is present in these images is what should be feared, yes, but also the ingredients of a desirable world: signed language and the shared knowledge of Deaf people—what Veditz calls "their thoughts and souls, their feelings, desires, and needs." These images

are not accidentally chosen. Stories like these are preserved for two reasons: they are carriers of history,
ways of repeating and reformulating the past or the
present, and they are vital means of teaching the wisdom of the group to those who do not have Deaf families. They are purposely, perhaps subconsciously,
chosen to pass on the group's knowledge about ways
of being.

IV. Topic: Identification & marginalization

Purpose: To help the student understand how Deaf
people categorize themselves and others, the language
they use to do so, and how the boundaries of their culture are defined.

Required reading:

Carol Padden & Tom Humphries. Deaf in America:
   Voices from a Culture. 1988. Cambridge, MA: Harvard University Press. Chapter 3.

Leo Jacobs. A Deaf Adult Speaks Out. 1974. Washington, DC: Gallaudet College Press. Chapter 7.

Content notes:

What does the sign DEAF represent? Not the English
word but the sign as it is taken from ASL when a Deaf
person identifies himself or another person with this
label. It represents a central, focal point for defining
oneself and from which others can be defined and
placed. Someone represented by the sign label HARD-
OF-HEARING is attributed a different history, experience, and identity than the one the label DEAF represents. These are not English labels but sign labels, and

as such align people in some way. This is the process of identifying and marginalizing that people of cultures adopt to know who share the same knowledge and way of being and to categorize those who may not.

Sometimes one can understand better what DEAF represents by understanding what it does not represent. It does not include a concept of disability, for one thing. Disabled is not a label or self-concept that has historically belonged to Deaf people. "Disabled" is a way of representing yourself, and it implies goals that are unfamiliar to Deaf people. Deaf people's enduring concerns have been these: finding each other and staying together, preserving their language, and maintaining lines of transmittal of their culture. These are not the goals of disabled people. Deaf people do know, however, the benefits of this label and make choices about alignment with these people politically.

This perception explains to some extent Deaf people's feelings about peddlers. Sometimes peddlers are treated as a political issue, as Arthur Roberts, president of the National Fraternal Society of the Deaf, did in the "Frat Magazine" in 1948; or they are treated as an economic issue as a Ms. Collums did in 1950. (Both from Padden & Humphries.) Roberts and many of the officials of Deaf organizations believed that Deaf people's difficulties came from a public image of them as lazy and dependent. They believed that eliminating peddlers [usually individuals who hand strangers a dog-eared card depicting the manual alphabet and ask for money] would change society's view of Deaf people. This was a political choice of images to use in trying to get every Deaf person to be individually responsible for maintaining an appropriate image before the public. Peddlers still represent the tension Deaf people feel about their public image. In *Tales from a Clubroom* (Bergman & Bragg; in Padden & Humphries), which was staged in 1980-81, one character is a peddler and he gives us an idea of the kind of justification peddlers use to politicize the act of peddling: that they are just getting back what hearing people took from them.

Whatever the justification, the image of "peddler" is counter to how Deaf people see themselves or how others see them. Peddlers are often said to come from the ranks of what Jacobs calls "the average deaf person;" and he identifies nine other categories of deaf people:

- adventitiously deaf adults
- prelingually deaf adults who come from deaf families
- other prelingually deaf adults
- low-verbal deaf adults
- uneducated deaf adults
- products of oral programs
- products of public schools
- deafened adults
- hard-of-hearing adults

When in English we say someone is an average American, we are conferring upon that one a kind of normality. "Average deaf adult" in ASL means something else entirely. It suggests someone "simple" or lacking in knowledge of the world. Jacobs says these are people who have been victimized, they suffer because of poor education or poor child rearing. This is a common belief, that the average deaf person is likely to be victimized in this way.

The label L-V (Jacobs' "low-verbal") is used for those without education but also for low-income ethnic minorities. Another term for these people is NOT SMART. Jacobs says of them that they "missed ... a great deal of education that they should have received" and are almost illiterate. It is common to believe that many peddlers are L-Vs who were manipulated into this by "King peddlers." The label refers primarily to educational characteristics but is also used to refer to the working poor and the chronically unemployed.

There is a lot to learn by asking questions about what Jacobs means by his other labels. What does he mean by "prelingually" deaf? What language is referred to there? Why does Jacobs distinguish between prelingually deaf of deaf families and others prelingually deaf? What does he say about prelingually deaf of deaf families?

With DEAF as the center, HARD-OF-HEARING people walk a thin line between being Deaf people who can do hearing things and being Deaf people who are too much like hearing people. There are other categories of people that help us to understand what the center is and is not. For example, ORAL people and ORAL FAIL people are people believed to have made incorrect life choices and suffer for it. Both can be quite insulting terms.

Stories about #EX ORAL people are popular. There is a variation of the Cinderella story that is told often and involves not magic slippers but magic gloves, which change a non-signing deaf woman into a signing Deaf woman and vastly improve her life.

THINK-HEARING is a newer term; it is just as insulting as ORAL but can be used to label any Deaf person, even those who are not ORAL. It is basically a term used to say that someone thinks like a hearing person.

Getting further from the center, DEAF, what about Deaf people's categorization of people under the term HEARING? There are many different and subtle categories in the culture for hearing people; some of these and ways of signing them are very specific:

- HEARING
- HEARING, BUT USES–SIGN–LANGUAGE
- HEARING, BUT SUPPORT–DEAF
- HEARING, DEAF PARENTS
- HEARING, DEAF BROTHER/SISTER
- HEARING, BUT SOCIALIZES–HEAVILY–WITH DEAF
- HEARING, SUPPORT–ORAL
- HEARING, SIGN S-E-E

What do these categories tell us about Deaf people? They seem to show that hearing people can be categorized according to levels of integration. But HEARING is not just a category of people who hear; it is a category of those who are the opposite of what Deaf people are; e.g. students at schools for Deaf children sometimes call their football opponents HEARING even when the team is from another school for Deaf children. (Padden & Humphries). All these ways of identifying and marginalizing are ways of aligning in relation to a center.

V. Topic: Hearing children in Deaf families

Purpose: To further refine the sense of the boundaries of the Deaf cultural group by examining the place in of children who hear.
Required reading: None
Additional material: Video, *Dim Sum*.

Content notes:

Dim Sum is a movie on video about Americans of Chinese descent. While the movie is not about Deaf people in any way, there is a certain parallelism between the patterns of behavior, family relationships, socialization, and language that is useful in setting the stage for discussion of hearing children born into Deaf families. When watching the movie it is interesting to watch for patterns of both language switching and cultural switching, to not any roles people assume, and the kinds of conflicts that arise.

Three generations of Americans of Chinese descent in the movie are represented by the mother and her friend the bar owner, the daughter and her friends, and the children of the daughter's generation. The three represent differing degrees of assimilation into both Chinese and American culture. The mother is still very much Chinese, although she is more Americanized than she first appears. The daughter is very much bicultural. The children of the third generation are more American than Chinese. The daughter is the focus of the movie, but there are several points to make:

The daughter, as a bicultural person, tries to accommodate both cultures. She feels the demands of both and the attraction of both and switches into either effortlessly. She does seem to have to make choices at times. Another point to make is about the interplay of languages. Some characters switch without any difficulty; some understand more than they are able to speak, and some are not able to switch.

Such is the situation with hearing children in Deaf families. The degree of assimilation into the culture of Deaf people varies greatly. Some hearing children in this situation grow up very active in the world of their parents and their community. Others grow up interacting only with the family and the world of hearing people.

The degree of bilinguality also varies greatly; many children are native in ASL, while many others understand ASL well but don't sign it very well; others do neither.

The degree of identification with one culture or the other varies greatly also. Many hearing children in Deaf families have a sense of duty or obligation (like the daughter in *Dim Sum*) to accommodate both cultures.

We can understand better how firm the boundaries are of the Deaf cultural group by examining the place of hearing children. Padden and Humphries in Chapter 3 report a common occurrence in sports competitions of the American Athletic Association of the Deaf, which has a rule that only *deaf* people can compete. As the story often goes, a Deaf teacher will allow a hearing child of Deaf parents to play, trying to sneak him in. When caught, it is often with great reluctance that the player is banned. Hearing children of Deaf parents have blood ties to Deaf people, as well as knowledge of the customs and language of the group. However, in matters that really count, they are not considered Deaf people.

At the same time it should be evident from the AAAD story that Deaf people will go to great lengths to accommodate these hearing children who have blood ties. Another example comes from the debate in the 1850s among people who were arguing whether to propose a Deaf state in the Union. One of the arguments against it that was used very effectively was: What do we do with hearing children of Deaf families? Someone suggested keeping them until they were of age then sending them out of the state. Others suggested that they be married to Deaf daughters. There was in this debate some evidence of the struggle to accommodate these people, but also those who used the argument clearly understood that the question of what to do about the hearing children would be hard for their opponents to answer and used it very effectively.

The variation in degree of assimilation into the Deaf cultural group that can be found among hearing children of Deaf families is a function of the choices that Deaf families make about the socialization of their hearing children. These choices are greatly influenced by social pressures. There is both a pressure for them to be Deaf and to be hearing, and whatever choices the parents make about the amount of cultural and language exposure the child will have will determine the degree of assimilation. This is not to suggest that there is ambiguity about hearing children of Deaf families among Deaf people. They clearly understand that hearing children of Deaf families hear, but they also understand that they must and can be accommodated in certain ways.

VI. Topic: Object & symbol

Purpose: To understand more completely the role of ASL in Deaf people's lives and to see how the meaning of ASL has changed for Deaf people.

Required reading:

Carol Padden & Tom Humphries. *Deaf in America: Voices from a Culture*. 1988. Cambridge, MA: Harvard University Press. Chapter 5

Leo Jacobs. *A Deaf Adult Speaks Out*. 1974. Washington, DC: Gallaudet University Press. Chapter 7.

Additional materials:

1. Videotape: *My Third Eye*
2. Film: *Charles Krauel: Profile of a Deaf Filmmaker*

Content notes:

As Geertz writes, we need to find the important symbols and understand their meaning in order to understand the people. We can begin with one of the most important elements of Deaf people's existence, American Sign Language. ASL's importance will become apparent in this unit and in the units to follow, as the theme of sign language appears again and again in various forms.

Of course it wasn't called American Sign Language or ASL until relatively recently. Many still refer to it as "sign language" or "sign," and there are many older Deaf people who will refer to it as "the sign language." There is even some reluctance to embrace the new name ASL because of the new ideology that surrounds this label. Although the label ASL is quickly becoming almost universally accepted, it is also filled with new meaning. It represents the history of social change that made it possible to think about Deaf people in terms of language and culture. A comparison of how ASL was used in performances of the past with the way it has been used in more recent performances reveals the extent to which it has become a subject of discussion and a symbol of certain ideologies. For example, the use of ASL in signed songs seen in the home movies of Charles Krauel (see film) and a video *The LACD Story*, shows Deaf signers to be very little conscious of ASL as an object to be noted; the performers seem to be very creative with the language but do not draw attention to the language itself. In contrast, the performers of the National Theatre of the Deaf in a more recent work, *My Third Eye*, actually remark that they are going to show and tell about their language, ASL, and proceed to pick out elements of its morphology to show the world.

An analysis of modern sign poetry by such poets as Dorothy Miles, Clayton Valli, and Ella Mae Lentz shows quite clearly the experience these poets have had with ASL as an object of analysis. Each of them shows an awareness of ASL structure in their work; e.g. "Total Communication" (Miles), "Windy Bright Morning" (Valli), and "Eye Music" (Lentz). They play with the structure of the language, e.g. the interaction of handshape and location, to an extent that shows their contemplation of ASL and how it works.

VII. Topic: The writings of Deaf people

Purpose: To explore the writings of Deaf people's lives for theme, symbol, and patterns of thought.
Required reading:

Eugene Bergman & Bernard Bragg. Tales from a Club-
    room. 1981. Washington, DC; Gallaudet University
    Press. Pp. 15-18, 22ff, 36-39, 58f, 113.

Shanny Mow. "How do you dance without music?" In
    Jacobs, *A Deaf Adult Speaks Out*. 1974. Reprinted in
    S. Wilcox, *American Deaf Culture*. Silver Spring, MD:
    Linstok Press, 1989.

Poems from *Manus*, literary magazine of T*he Buff &*
    Blue, student newspaper of Gallaudet College (Uni-
    versity).

Content notes:

What is the place of writing (in English) in the culture
of Deaf people? Writing is used by Deaf people in
many situations: to communicate with hearing people
who do not sign, for letters and notes, in their profes-
sions and work places, for artistic expression, and in
TTY/TDD conversations—to name just a few. There is
clearly a role for written forms of English in the culture.
But like everything else, writing is part of a complex
web of meaning and rules for use. Knowing the place
of writing in the culture is important, but it is also what
is expressed through writing that is particularly reveal-
ing of values and patterns of thought of the people who
do the writing. In these writings may be found themes
that are important to Deaf people, messages about
what the people hold to be valuable, liturgies of frus-
trations and satisfactions of the writer, and often patterns of thought that reveal a type of consciousness.

There are several ways we can analyze Deaf people's writings. We can do a thematic analysis, merely
identifying themes in the text. A thematic analysis of

poems found in a few issues of *Manus* reveals the following recurring themes:

- Sign language is important to the education of Deaf children (Schreiber)
- Sign language is essential to express oneself (Schreiber, Kalb, Garretson)
- Deaf people's love for their language (Driedger)
- Being Deaf as a state of normality, centrality, and harmony (Hanson)
- Problems with "others" (hearing people) (Taylor)
- Deaf people have their own way of seeing things (Garretson)
- The importance of Deaf control (Garretson)
- Oppression (Garretson)
- Deaf people as human (Hanson, Garretson)
- ASL as an art (Rothenberg)

Analysis of the frustration-satisfaction theme in Shanny Mow's poem, which lists expressions of each state, reveals a very detailed picture of Deaf people's negative experience within a world of hearing "others" and the satisfaction they draw from their own group.

A thematic analysis of the play *Tales from a Clubroom* reveals these themes: problems with hearing others' oppression (22ff), ignorance of the "oral world" and revenge against hearing "others" (36-39), the place of hearing children of Deaf parents (58f), revenge against hearing "others" again (113). But these are only a few of the themes to be found in this play.

One can also look for symbols or metaphor to represent certain things such as sign language. In a group of poems from *Manus*, are the following symbols for 'signing': a ballet, light to eyes, a bright moon on a peaceful night, and waves rolling into shore. In such analysis of these poems and other writings can be found the voice of the culture.

VIII. Topic: Oral literature

Purpose: To understand the tradition of "oral" literature and language arts that carry the history and teaching of Deaf people across generations.

Required reading:

Rutherford, S. Funny in deaf—not in hearing, *Journal of American Folklore* 96: 381. 1983.

Frishberg, N. Signers of tales: A case for literary status of an unwritten language, *Sign Language Studies* 59. 1988.

Additional materials:

1. Film: National Association of the Deaf film series, including "The Preservation of the Sign Language" and "The Irishman and the Flea."

2. Video: The San Francisco Library *Deaf Culture Series.*

3. *The World According to Pat: Reflections of Residential School Days*, by Pat Graybill. Sign Media, Inc.

Content notes:

If there are universal patterns of behavior among cultures, one of them is that groups of people pass down the knowledge and beliefs which they deem important to the survival and quality of life of future generations of their descendents. The collective memory of a group of people (the knowledge they wish to retain and share with others) has various forms. Language is one of these forms, a language is an organization of symbols which people pass down to future generations. Language also is used as a medium to carry knowledge and beliefs. Sometimes a group devises a writing system and this becomes another tool for preservation and transmission of knowledge. Or a group will devise a tradition of storytelling and "oral" history in which important knowledge and recipes for living are passed from person to person "orally" or, in the case of Deaf people, by signing.

Because the "oral" tradition of Deaf people is not very well documented or explained, it is easy to overlook this important aspect of Deaf people's lives. Also, since Deaf people do write in English, there is a mixture of this "oral" tradition and a tradition of writing in English which Deaf people have used. In this century, documentation of the "oral" tradition has been more possible through the use of film and videotape but it has not been done to a great extent because such efforts are still more to preserve than to actually pass on the message. It is the message, however, in the stories, sermons, lectures, preaching, jokes, songs, poetry, and so forth which tells us about the people who perpetuate the culture and the tradition.

Earlier we saw the story of a Deaf man, Joshua Davis, and his brush with death and salvation by his connection to other Deaf people. This is an excellent example of a story which has been told many times, varying slightly in detail over a hundred years. It is a family story that clearly has a message that Deaf people feel is important. The lecture, "The Preservation of the Sign Language," by George Veditz in the 1913 film series made by the NAD is an example of the kind of "oral" history that is told and retold, the story of the Abbé de l' Epée, the banning of signed language in Europe in 1880, the hardship of Deaf people without signed language in the school, and the blessing of American Deaf people who can use signed language in their schools. All of these ingredients are constantly repeated in many forms in many different ways in the "talk" of Deaf people.

Since residential schools are so central to Deaf people's lives as places where Deaf people find each other, there is a strong tradition of storytelling and other forms of literature which relates, recounts, and romanticizes life in these schools. Examples of such texts performed by Pat Graybill can be found among the tapes of "The World According to Pat: Reflections of Residential School Days."

Jokes, such as the "Please but" joke (see Rutherford) and the "motel joke" (see Padden & Humphries) are examples of the use of humor to describe experiences or imaginary experiences and to share perceptions of a sensitive nature in a permissible form. Stories of residential school life tell of the socialization process among deaf children and the strong ties Deaf people establish with each other and their schools as well as the role the world of the school plays in the cultural development of the children who live there.

Sources such as these and public performances today of poetry, storytelling, and drama in American

Sign Language show us the vibrancy of the "oral" literature of Deaf people.

IX. Topic: Theme and symbol in art

Purpose: To present some of the art and artists of the American Deaf community and explore theme and symbol in this art.

Required reading:

Gannon, J. *Deaf Heritage: A Narrative History of Deaf America.*

Silver Spring, MD.: National Association of the Deaf.

Additional materials: Slides of the artwork to be presented.

Content notes:

Several Deaf artists and their work explore themes and use symbols which tell us something about the artist and his/her experience. Some of these common themes and symbols are:

- oppression of language (Betty Miller)
- oppression by educators & society (Betty Miller, Harry Williams)
- world of vision (Igor Kolombatovic, Robert Roth, Morris Broderson, Betty Miller, Harry Williams)
- signs and fingerspelling (Broderson, Williams, Betty Miller)
- hands and eyes (Betty Miller, John Brewster)

Not all works of art by Deaf artists so clearly communicate or interpret the experience of being Deaf in the United States. Other visual artists of particular note are: Cadwallader Washburn, Felix Kowalewski, and Douglas Tilden, whose monumental sculptures are to be found in the San Francisco area.

The issue of what constitutes Deaf art is often debated but is probably more a reflection of the debate about what constitutes Deaf culture than of whether there are Deaf artists and whether they have something to express. There is Deaf art because there are Deaf artists and they, of course, do have something to express whether it is their experience as Deaf people in the United States or whether it is an expression of the human condition. Deaf artists have done and do both.

X. Topic: Living within others' worlds

Purpose:

1. To explore the relationship between Deaf people and the worlds of others.
2. To understand what kinds of theories Deaf people have about themselves and about others.
3. To learn how the knowledge of Deaf people and the "science" of others diverge and converge.

Required reading:

Padden, C. & T. Humphries. *Deaf in America: Voices from a*

Culture. 1988. Cambridge: Mass. Harvard University Press. Chapter 5.

Content notes:

Deaf people have always lived within other people's worlds. Their local communities are located within larger communities of people who hear and use a different language. What does this mean for Deaf people? How does it show up in the ways Deaf people talk about and explain things? We are now at the problem that Deaf people have of developing and holding an independent understanding of themselves while living in a world surrounded by others who have a different theory about them, in fact, a "science of deafness."

This divergence between the theory that Deaf people have about themselves and the one that others have held about them is most evident in theories about their signed language. Non-Deaf people have written extensively about "sign language" (see reference to Myklebust in Padden & Humphries) and up until two decades ago, had not considered it a language nor a phenomenon worthy of any further research other than a superficial observation. Certainly, no rigorous linguistic study was ever attempted. The theory that others had about Deaf people's signed language basically defined it as a crutch and a secondary system of communication which was a last resort when Deaf people failed to learn English.

Faced with these kinds of opinion of others about their signed language, what kinds of theories did Deaf people themselves develop about their language? An examination of letters and editorials in the *Silent Worker*, the forerunner to the *Deaf American* reveals some of the ways Deaf people thought about their language. On one hand, they acknowledged the theory of others that it was "not a language" but on the other hand, referred to it as "natural," "pleasing to see," and as having "a correct form of delivery." This contradictory way of talking about their language reveals their attempts to reconcile two very powerful realities: sign language is rejected by the larger society but is the most essential thing Deaf people have. Deaf people developed two ways of talking about the language to avoid conflict between the two theories. This is typical of the strategy Deaf people have used to live with the contradictory theories of others about them.

The play *Tales from a Clubroom* has scenes that show the tension within the community of Deaf people about the ideas and behaviors of others when they find their way into the group. One such scene revolves around the character of Lindsey who signs some form of signed English, leading members of the club to misunderstand and resent him and think of him as being a snob who is pretending to be better than they are. Other scenes in the play which indicate the competition between the theory Deaf people have of themselves and the theory held by others include: scenes in which Lindsey and the bartender, Shalleck, each an archtype, compete for the attention of the same woman; a discussion about the acceptability and justifiability of "peddling;" and, the "frog joke." Deaf people find the "science" of others about their signed language and culture to be inadequate and sometimes false. Living with these theories of others while maintaining separate theories of themselves is a testament of the inventiveness of the culture.

XI. Topic: Appropriation of ASL for pedagogical sign

systems

Purpose:

1. To better understand Deaf people's view of ASL and other signing behavior derived from ASL.

2. To explore some of the research into these derived sign systems.

Required reading:

Baker, C. "How does 'sim-com' fit into a bilingual approach to education?" *Proceedings National Symposium on Sign Language Research & Teaching*. 1978. Silver Spring, MD: National Association of the Deaf.

Additional reading:

Kluwin, T. "The grammaticality of manual representations of English in classroom settings". *American Annals of the Deaf*, June, 1981.

Supalla, S.1991. "Manually coded English: The modality question in signed language development." In *Issues in Sign Language Research: Psychology*, Siple & Susan Fischer, eds. Chicago: University of Chicago Press.

Content notes:

Deaf people have particular ideas about their language. Often these ideas have been challenged by others as we have seen. Intuitive and practical knowledge about signed language which Deaf people hold often conflict with suggestions of others as to what can and cannot be done with signed language. If one talked to

Deaf people about a signed English system ("SEE" as these systems are often called), one will get a range of responses but often one will get, "It doesn't feel right;" or "It's okay but it's for use in school only." Lately, the acceptability of such signed English systems has become so politicized as to become a litmus test for anyone wanting to be politically correct. Why doesn't it "feel right?" Why isn't it for everyday use, or why is it, as Krauel implies, unnatural?

Some studies may explain to some extent the constraints on such systems which contribute to Deaf people's intuition about them. A study by Baker (see reading) indicates what happens when one tries to speak English and sign at the same time, comparing the speaking and signing rates per minute and the number and types of grammatical deletions that occur in signing when using forms of "manual English." Her thesis is that with the constraints on signing and on speaking and on understanding either, something has to give.

A study by Kluwin indicates that the more experienced SEE signers who would be expected to more perfectly adhere to SEE actually adopt more ASL–like features as time goes by, raising questions about the efficiency of SEE in communication even for the most experienced signers of it. Supalla argues in another study that spoken languages cannot be incorporated into a signed medium and argues further that it is because of the modality constraints, not constraints on what signed languages can do morphologically or syntactically. He argues that language acquisition patterns for both the visual modality and auditory modality are the same as demonstrated by other studies. Thus, modality does not affect acquisition of a natural language. But because the children he studied did not mimic the adult models of SEE they were exposed to but rather transformed what they saw individually into other forms, he argues that they are acting out modality constraints.

These studies help us to understand Deaf people's feelings about their language, ASL, and their concerns about what is happening with "manual English" in a context outside of their cultural perceptions. This research seems to verify what Deaf people know. The irony is that the "science" of others is beginning to restructure itself to recognize what Deaf people have known.

XII. Topic: Ownership of sound

Purpose: To explore the meaning of sound and the relationship of Deaf people to sound.

Required reading:

Padden, C. & T. Humphries. *Deaf in America: Voices from a*

Culture. 1988. Cambridge: Mass. Harvard University Press. Chapter 6.

Content notes:

A widespread misconception about Deaf people is that they live in a world without sound. For hearing people, the world becomes known through sound. So they end up believing that Deaf people are condemned to a life lacking the depth of meaning that sound makes available to hearing people. Sound is more than acoustics.

Sound is known through meaning as well (see reading). In any discussion of Deaf people's knowledge of sound, it is important to keep in mind that perception of sound is not automatic or straightforward, but shaped through learned, culturally defined practices. Within a culture, it is as important to know the specific and special meaning of sound as it is to hear sound.

Many Deaf people know a great deal about sound, and sound--not just its absence—plays a central role in their lives. Examples (from the reading) can be found in the recreation of movies in sign with sound effects, a game which many Deaf adults recall playing in the dorms when they were in school and in other games such as competitions to see which could yell the loudest and others which seem designed to annoy their teachers. These types of activities involving experimenting with and playing with sound are not isolated incidents but are part of a tradition passed down from one generation to the next. They are part of the process of learning about the properties of sound and about how volume and resonance works.

These experiments and others are also sometimes the beginning of learning about how hearing people think about sound. Deaf people, living among hearing people as they do, figure out the complicated meaning system attached to various sounds which hearing people share. The politeness system attached to sound such as the meaning of a burp (see reading) is just one small part of this complicated system. Such meaning is sometimes confusing to Deaf people but not any more so than to other hearing people of other cultures.

Deaf people also learn about the control of sound. A great deal of the interaction between Deaf and hearing people revolves around sound and the control of it. There are stories and jokes about how Deaf people suffer at the hands of others because of others' control of sound. Often these stories tell how Deaf people take control of sound and turn the tables on hearing people (see reading).

When hearing people speculate about Deaf people's lives the absence of sound in the form of music often strikes them as a serious lessening of the quality of life for Deaf people. People who hear have difficulty imagining a satisfactory life without music. However, harmony, variation, resonance, dissonance, counterpoint, etc. are all characteristics of music that are not limited to sound. Deaf people find similar characteristics in movement, and they are able to organize movement into something meaningful in the same way that music is composed. In poems such as those of Clayton Valli and Ella Lentz (see reading), all of these characteristics and more are used. This is not to suggest that these movements and organization of movements are replacements for sound. Sound is not absent from Deaf people's lives, so Deaf people are not replacing it with movement.

Deaf people instead are using their own resources to explore the same complicated creative realm that hearing people—endeavoring to organize sound and create music—often think of as uniquely theirs. Deaf people create their world around the resources of movement, form, and sound. Silence as a metaphor for explaining Deaf people's lives is therefore clumsy and inadequate; it explains more what is central in hearing people's lives (i.e. sound) than what is central in Deaf people's lives.

XIII. Topic: Political manifestations of ethnicity

Purpose: To understand the nature of the bond between Deaf people and the political ways that this bond is maintained and projected.

Required reading:

Flournoy, J. J. and others. Selected letters from the *American Annals of the Deaf*. 1855-1858.

Content notes:

To understand the nature of the bond between Deaf people, one must understand ethnicity. Geertz characterizes ethnic groups as bound together by what he calls "primordial attachments" or the givens of existence including kinship, language, and custom. This is not just some personal affection or common interest that binds people together, but something stronger that seems to come from a natural affinity for humans to be attracted to each other. This bond between people within an ethnic group tends to be politicized with the result that an ethnic group has two aims: (1) to be recognized and (2) to improve the quality of life for themselves.

As a group, Deaf people have had these aims and have manifested these aims in political ideas and actions over the years. Probably the most startling example of this in history is the proposal by J. J. Flournoy in 1856 to establish a state for Deaf people somewhere in the west. The reason Flournoy stated for doing this was: "... our peculiar necessities and such arrangements as may be indispensable to our welfare, are not known or provided for;" and so Deaf people needed "a political independence, a state sovereignty."

There was an exchange of letters regarding this proposal in the *American Annals of the Deaf* over a period of two or three years with various people writing to support or argue against the idea. This debate reveals much of what binds Deaf people together and the tension within the group. Some arguments for the state were:

- Deaf people's abilities are not limited by not hearing.
- Deaf people are superior to the *mad* hearing legislators.
- In our own state, we can attain the dignity and honor of Human nature.
- A Deaf commonwealth Constitution can guarantee power for Deaf to rule hearing.
- Hearing children can leave when ready as they do in the general population.
- The commonwealth will allow the pleasure and improvement Deaf get from society with each other.
- We learn best from each other--hearing people are burdened conversing with us.
- No point in just a settlement if hearing still rule--need political independence.
- Hearing families keep Deaf at home like "lap-dogs" and hearing will keep Deaf in everlasting childhood.
- Attention to us is based upon inferior considerations; when we claim equality, it offends hearing people.
- A deaf-mute government is the very best institution we can establish.

- We would allow no martial arms; neither a slave state nor a state where free Negroes are admitted.
- Even if we fail, still prove we are capable of many things.
- Laurent Clerc himself first proposed this idea.

Arguments against the separate state included:

- Unwillingness to break ties of family.
- If poor, no means to move; if wealthy, no motivation to leave present place.
- What will be done with hearing children.
- If a Deaf person is unhappy, must look within himself for the cause.
- We don't need a state, can just get together and live together without a new government.
- Deaf people will engage in scandal, backbiting, and other diabolisms.
- Government of a state would be an inconvenient responsibility.
- The majority of Deaf people show little decisiveness of purpose in any enterprise.
- Sparsely settled state would make nobody rich; couldn't prevent selling land to hearing people.
- Deaf people will read more if left scattered across the country.
- People will be homesick.

Even some of the opposition, including Edwin Booth and Edward Fay, proposed similar ideas, though these ideas were for settlements rather than politically independent states. Many of the letters made personal attacks on Flournoy's character as a way to discredit his proposal. Though no state was actually attempted, this debate is a rich study of the ethnic aims of recognition and improvement.

What is the form of Deaf people's current drive to provide for their "peculiar necessities?" A couple of examples are the "of, by, and for" community activism in California and the Gallaudet University civil disturbance to force a Deaf presidency.

XIV. Topic: Possible lives

Purpose:

1. To gain some insight into Deaf people's images of what constitute "possible" lives for themselves.

2. To understand Deaf people's ideas about integration with others.

Required reading:

Padden, C. & T. Humphries. *Deaf in America: Voices from a*

Culture. 1988. Cambridge, MA: Harvard University Press. Chapter 6.

Content notes:

Flournoy proposed a separatist idea which received negative response from many Deaf people. In the end,

the proposal was probably too separatist for it to suc-
ceed. Deaf people's notion of lives for themselves probably does not include this kind of drastic separation
from hearing people, many of whom are related to
them by blood. At the same time, integration as proposed by others is different in goal and in practice from
that envisioned by Deaf people. The problem with proposals by others for integration of Deaf people is that
they do not conform with what Deaf people consider to
be "possible" lives. Many of the stories and other texts
we have discussed in this course indicate what are
"possible" and what are "not possible" lives for Deaf
people: the young Deaf woman drowning in the NTD
play, Joshua Davis saved from hanging, children's
play with sound, and Krauel's film record.

Another very good example is the Robert McGregor story filmed in 1913 (see Padden & Humphries),
"The Irishman and the Flea." The story mocks the oral-
ist's ideal of a "restored–to–society deaf," or a Deaf
person who is just like hearing people. He makes it
clear that such a person will "never" be found. His
message is that it is impossible for a Deaf person to be
a hearing person. His story disparages the longing of
hearing people to shape Deaf people into people who
do not seem deaf at all. McGregor does not accept the
kind of integration that has the Deaf person becoming
something else or becoming indistinguishable from
hearing people. Integration with others for Deaf people
is coexistence and interactive but not assimilative.

Geertz says that culture is how we "complete ourselves." In theory, there are many cultures of the world
and we learn the one to which we are exposed, fulfilling the innate search for culture in all. But what if there

are cultures that have evolved from generations of people of a particular set of physical characteristics when along comes an individual with a different set of physical characteristics? Perhaps not all cultures, then, are compatible with all individuals. Some cultures may not be fully accessible to some, as is the case of deaf people and hearing cultures. In many Deaf cultures of the world deaf people will be comfortable. These cultures represent what Deaf people believe to be "possible" lives for themselves. And these "possible" lives have at least one thing in common. They are all historically created lives. That is, they evolve over generations of Deaf people and are learned by each new generation of Deaf children. It is by these lives that Deaf people can complete themselves.

Why America Needs Deaf Culture: Cultural Pluralism and the Liberal Arts Tradition

Stephen Wilbers
University of Minnesota

At the conclusion of Ralph Ellison's *Invisible Man*, the narrator retreats to the hole of his basement, where he wires the entire ceiling, every square inch of it, with 1,368 lightbulbs. There, brilliantly illuminated yet invisible to the outside world, he contemplates the irony of his existence. A black man in white America, suffering from the ultimate humiliation: non-existence. After some twenty years of searching for his black American identity, the invisible man discovers that in the eyes of white America, mainstream America, he simply does not exist.

His dilemma is analogous to the condition of Deaf culture in America today. In the minds of many hearing Americans, the deaf community simply does not exist. While prejudice may be a factor in this perception, the cause, I believe, runs deeper. It has to do with how we see ourselves as Americans. It has to do with our traditional assumptions about who we are as a people, about how we define our national identity. And it has to do with our feelings and thoughts about diversity, about people and cultures that differ from the mainstream.

As citizens of a nation characterized by racial and cultural diversity from its beginnings, we have responded to our cultural dissimilarity basically in three ways. According to historian Russell Menard (1986:2), two of them, Anglo-conformity and the ideal of the melting pot, "stressed assimilation, usually ignored non-Europeans, and appeared early in American history." The third, pluralism, is a more recent phenomenon. Rather than assimilation, it celebrates diversity and "at least in some version escapes the Eurocentrism of Anglo-conformity and the melting pot by recognizing the key role of blacks, Indians, Hispanics, and Asians in American life" (Menard, 1986:2).

In the 1960s the Eurocentric assumptions and assimilationist thinking of Anglo-conformist and melting pot theorists were "forcefully challenged, first by blacks and later by Native Americans, Asian Americans, and Hispanics" (Menard, 1986:3). Menard (ibid.:4) explains how this challenge came to be reflected in the university curriculum:

> Scholars, many of them veterans of the civil rights movement, more of them moved by the struggles of minority groups for justice and recognition, became increasingly sensitive to the diversity of the American experience and incorporated that concern into their research and teaching.... By the mid-1970's, a pluralist approach to the American experience had established a secure place in the university curriculum. Courses across the curriculum recognized the persistent diversity of American culture and went beyond the Eurocentric vision of earlier formulations to acknowledge

the key role of people of color in U.S. history and
life.

In some ways, this change came as an obvious and
natural transition. Traditionally, liberal education has
been associated with breadth in learning. As Jerry G.
Gaff (1983:7) reminds us in *General Education Today*,
one of the widely accepted attributes of general education as a curriculum is that it "provides students with
familiarity with various branches of human understanding as well as the methodologies and languages
particular to different bodies of knowledge." To recognize American cultural diversity and declare it a body
of knowledge suitable for academic inquiry, then, was
not a particularly radical departure.

My argument in this article is that the time has
come for American higher education to take the next
logical step. The time has come for us to extend this
same notion of pluralistic recognition and inquiry to
the language and culture of the deaf community.

One might even note that, compared to ethnic cultures in American society, Deaf culture offers a unique
feature. Like gender, it cuts across all racial and economic lines. One illustration of this is the fact that deaf
children (of whom over 90% are born to hearing parents) commonly include in their concept of "family"
their teachers and deaf schoolmates as well as their
parents and relatives. Deaf culture is unique in the
sense that it overlays segments of other subcultures
and redefines traditional social boundaries and entities. As such, it offers special challenges and opportunities to the student of language and culture.

In considering the rationale for including Deaf culture and language in the liberal arts curriculum, it may

be useful to remind ourselves of the educational purposes of foreign or second language study generally. In
his introductory essay to this volume, Paul Chapin
identifies three:

1. to provide an opportunity for the student
   to learn "to understand language as a
   structured system" (which leads the student "to a fuller appreciation of the structure of his own native language")

2. to give the student entree into another culture, and thus to broaden his perspective

3. to expose the student to a new, different
   mode of aesthetic expression.

According to Chapin, American Sign Language
(ASL) serves all three purposes admirably. In fact, the
study of ASL and American Deaf culture, he claims, offers the special advantages of immediacy:

> Unlike the great national cultures which the for-
> eign language student usually confronts, Ameri-
> can Deaf culture is among us, though typically
> invisible to hearing persons. Indeed, the very in-
> visibility is itself a strong argument for education
> and enlightenment of members of the majority
> culture.

In the spring of 1987 the University of Minnesota
took the step I am advocating. The College of Liberal
Arts recognized American Sign Language as one of the
languages students might study in fulfillment of its
second language requirement. When the Scholastic
Standing Committee began its investigation of Ameri-

can Sign Language the preceding fall, we addressed three basic questions:

1. Is ASL a language separate and distinct from English with a grammar, morphology, and syntax of its own?

2. Would the study of ASL provide students with the learning experience of entering linguistically a culture different from their own?

3. Would this field of study have opportunities for research and exploration comparable to those offered by the study of oral and written languages?

To all three questions, the Committee answered yes. In fact, the evidence provided by the experts, by linguists and other scholars, is overwhelming.[1] Through their research, they have confirmed what native users of ASL have known all along: that the language which is so vital and central to Deaf culture is every bit as complex and nuanced and capable of artistic expression as English.

The Committee felt strongly that the study of any natural language was a liberal pursuit, and consequently worthy of credit. In recommending that the College allow students to fulfill the Second Language Requirement with proficiency in ASL, the Committee was confident that students who did so would experience the rigors and pleasures of language study as rich-

---

[1] For more discussion of the arguments for including ASL in the liberal arts curriculum, see Stephen Wilbers (1987:4-9, 30); and Sherman Wilcox and Stephen Wilbers (1987).

ly as do students who choose an oral or written language.

The premise that a definable and viable Deaf culture exists is based on the fact that being Deaf involves more than not being able to hear. Being Deaf involves having a unique perspective on the world, one that differs in fundamental ways from the perspective of hearing people. As Jack Gannon, Susan Rutherford, Sherman Wilcox, and others have pointed out, Deaf people have their own values, allegiances, patterns of daily living, politics, folklore, and world view. As many people know, what is funny to a hearing person is not necessarily funny to a Deaf person, and vice – versa.

But do these values and this special way of perceiving the world constitute a Deaf culture?

Perhaps the best response to this question is to say that, if one defines culture as a pattern of values and beliefs used by a community of people to perceive and interpret their individual and collective experience, both past and present, then there is unquestionably a Deaf culture. If on the other hand culture is defined more narrowly in terms of the Western classical tradition, or is posited on the existence of a written literature, then it becomes more difficult to argue that Deaf culture is separate and distinct from mainstream American society. (For a full discussion of American Deaf culture, see Rutherford in this volume.)

Despite receiving three unanimous votes by faculty governance bodies on its way to winning final approval, our new policy has not gone unchallenged.[2] One of the better informed and more articulate dissenters was Faye Allen, whose maternal grandparents were profoundly deaf. (She and her sisters learned to communicate their needs and wants to them in fingerspelling and signs "long before we could use speech to get what we wanted from our parents.")

As director of the W. Roby Allen School in Faribault, Minnesota, which is an oral school started by her mother in 1923, Ms. Allen has devoted her entire life "to the education of deaf youngsters," and she takes issue with the change that exempts native ASL users from learning a foreign language. She worries that granting these exemptions shows "favoritism" for deaf students:

> Present day teaching is putting our faith in the education of deaf students with hearing students, meeting the identical requirements. May we wonder if at some future date this young man [who petitioned the College for exemption from learning a third language after ASL and English] will wish that he too might have known some French, German or Spanish?...
>
> Clerc taught and used the sign language over 150 years ago. The sign language and finger spelling

---

[2] The proposal, as it was finally endorsed by the College of Liberal Arts, includes four points. It:

1. recognizes ASL as a complete, natural language
2. accepts demonstration of six-quarter proficiency in ASL to meet the second-language requirement [we have a proficiency-based second-language requirement at Minnesota, with entrance and graduation proficiency exams required]
3. exempts native ASL users proficient in English from the second-language requirement [as we exempt native speakers of oral and written languages other than English]
4. accepts credit earned in college study of ASL toward the College's graduation credit requirement.

are as essential today as they were then. I always
use this means of communication in "talking" to
a deaf person who is not able to read lips. I am
glad I can and do think manually. But, we are
talking about allowing a non-hearing student to
deprive himself, legally, of exposure to another
language. The issue is not philosophy of teaching.
The issue is not asylums, schools, academics. The
young man is losing out in an area which is offered to enrich a student's life. Is the young man
against any and all other foreign languages or is
he working for a wider use of sign language in
the hearing world? I would like to know the real
purpose of his request.[3]

Ms. Allen explained to me that her deaf students
and adult friends "are sharing my surprise and shock
that a college student would ask for any exemption
from fulfilling the same requirements that are met by
all students working towards the same academic degree."[4] For her, the issue is a matter of pride in the abilities and accomplishments of her own deaf students, as
well as a statement of equal rights and equal treatment
for deaf people.

My response went along these lines.

Part of our motivation in allowing students to use
ASL to satisfy our second language requirement is indeed a desire to recognize the existence of a deaf community and a Deaf culture. In fact, I would argue that
the students who stand to gain the most are not the
handful of Deaf students at the University who might

---

[3] Faye Allen, in a letter to the author, date April 14, 1987.

[4] Ibid.

claim ASL as their first language and English as their second. (Of our 45,000 students on the Twin Cities campus, 24 are deaf and use interpreters.) On the contrary, I believe that those who might benefit most are the hearing students who through the study of ASL will encounter a rich and viable culture fundamentally different from their own. In this sense, the proposal opens the door for another whole area of study, one that promises to lead to new awareness and appreciation of the diversity that characterizes American society. Here our goal of expanding our students' grasp of the varieties of human experience is the same one that we set for the study of any natural language.

It is true that the few native users of ASL on our campus will no longer be required to master a third language after English, though as educators we will certainly continue to encourage them to do so. But it is our belief that this decision should be theirs to make, just as we do not require our international students to master a third language after English.

When viewed in this light, I would argue, the new policy represents more of an opportunity than a compromise. Just as Ms. Allen maintains that our deaf students have the same right to a quality degree as do hearing students, so I would argue that they have the same right to decide whether they want to study a third language or devote their time and effort to other pursuits. Our goal with all our students, whether hearing or deaf, is to help them achieve the appropriate balance between required and elective areas of study.

Beyond these academic considerations, one might ask: What are the practical effects of making the study of ASL and Deaf culture an established part of the liberal arts curriculum?

A good way to answer that question is to take a look at what is happening at Madonna College, a small, private liberal arts institutions in Livonia, Michigan. While Madonna has no foreign language requirement, it offers a B.A., an A.A. and a minor in sign language studies. With the enthusiastic support of Sister Francilene (who is one of the only college presidents in the country who can communicate in sign with deaf faculty, students, and parents), its sign language studies program has been conferred departmental status, which affords it institutional recognition. Furthermore, Kenneth Rust, Dennis Berigan, Michael Meldrum, and Mary Wells report that the department's office, strategically located just off one of the main lounges, has become a symbol of integration on campus.

With some 100 deaf students in a population of approximately 4000, Deaf culture has made its presence felt at Madonna in a way that has enriched the educational environment for all concerned. One unexpected benefit of having such a relatively high proportion of deaf students and interpreters in the classroom is that instructors, as a result of taking special care to make themselves understood, report improvement in the quality of their lecture style, delivery, and teaching methods generally.

I believe our hope as a nation lies in recognizing and accepting our cultural and racial diversity. We grow stronger not by demanding that everyone be melted into the same pot, not by insisting on total assimilation of every newcomer or every person who differs in some significant way from the majority, but by recognizing the unique and individual gifts that each cultural group brings to the whole. In other words, we want not only the taste but the texture of the chocolate chips in our cookies — or, if you prefer — the marsh-mallows in our hot chocolate.

I sometimes wonder, if a medical cure could be found for all deafness, would all hearing-impaired people avail themselves of the remedy? No doubt many would, but surely there would be some who would not. Whatever their decision, I suspect that nearly all would lament the breakup of a close-knit community, whose members know a great deal about caring and coping in a world too often unattuned to them.

America needs Deaf culture just as it needs Black culture, Asian culture, Hispanic culture, and Native American culture. We need to learn what these cultures have to teach us about their concepts of reality and their ways of perceiving the world. We need to be informed by their particular languages and enlightened by their art forms. And for their sake, we need to remember that there is perhaps no greater tragedy than to deny people their selfhood and sense of individual identity.

When I search for a metaphor for the deaf community that is comparable to Ellison's invisible man with his 1,369 lightbulbs, I imagine a troop of Deaf actors performing behind a closed curtain, or I imagine a Deaf storyteller in a darkened theater. I think we should do ourselves a favor. I think it's time we opened the curtain and turned up the lights.

References

Gaff, J. G. 1983. *General Education Today: A Critical Analysis of Controversies,* Practices, and Reforms. San Francisco, CA: Jossey-Bass Publishers.

Menard, R.R. 1986. Curricular Recognition of U.S. Cultural Diversity, *Papers on CLA Students,* a quarterly publication of the Office of the director, Student Academic Support Services, College of Liberal Arts, University of Minnesota, (Volume IV, No. 3).

Wilbers, S. 1987. The Case for Recognizing American Sign Language. *The College Board Review,* 145.

Wilcox, S. & S. Wilbers. 1987. The Case for Academic Acceptance of American Sign Language. Opinion, *The Chronicle of Higher Education,* July 1.

American Sign Language in the High School System

Peggy J. Selover

The topic of American Sign Language (ASL) in the high school system has garnered considerable positive response in recent years. The phrase I hear most often is, "I wish it had been offered when *I* was in high school." We can all relate to time spent in high school studying French, Spanish, perhaps Latin, and wondering when we'd ever use the language. With ASL it's a different story. You can converse within the boundaries of your own town or city.

Learning to communicate in another language so unlike those traditionally taught in our schools excites the student. This is new — and different. For such a captive audience, a wealth of knowledge awaits.

Through the medium of high school classes, ASL will spread easily through the hearing community. If each hearing person studying ASL and Deaf culture talks with just one other person about their studies, imagine the awareness spreading like wildfire. The inquisitive student will seek out deaf counterparts to talk with to learn more about deafness. Sensitivity, awareness, respect, understanding — that's what this is about.

As for deaf education, the deaf student has not previously been presented the opportunity to study her own language in high school. To many deaf individuals, the morphological and grammatical processes of ASL are as much a mystery as they are to hearing individuals. At long last, the deaf student will have a chance to excel in a foreign language; her own native language will be offered as a course of study. Classes in Deaf culture and artistic expression through ASL will further serve to enlighten and empower the deaf student.

Our hearing society has for years insidiously oppressed the deaf by taking over, "doing for," and "helping". In bringing ASL into the limelight, we present opportunities for empowerment of deaf individuals. We will see more deaf teachers in hearing high schools and colleges and more deaf role models which the students need in their lives. Also, as hearing people learn about deafness — the language and culture — they will feel less threatened when approached by deaf individuals. Ultimately, more jobs will be accessible to the deaf by virtue of better understanding.

And, of course, there's always the issue of mainstreaming to consider. If deaf students continue to be mainstreamed into hearing classrooms, they must be provided with "the least restrictive environment" as mandated by PL 94-142. The existing barrier for the deaf student is *communication*. A means of establishing free-flowing communication among hearing and deaf students must be provided in order to comply with the law.

In teaching ASL to high school students, we present the possibility for real communication among hearing students and those deaf and hearing impaired students mainstreamed into hearing environments.

I am the originator and sponsor of California Assembly Bill 51 (AB 51) which requires California high schools to give foreign language credit to American Sign Language courses. The idea for this legislation grew from my experiences with the Deaf community during the past ten years. I've seen the challenges which confront deaf citizens on a daily basis, and believe the communication barrier which exists between hearing and deaf persons is the largest obstacle to be overcome. This barrier prevents access to full participation and freedom by deaf people within society at large.

Why legislate rather than work through the educational hierarchy? It seemed more concrete to create a law than continue to bring the subject up for endless discussion. Fifteen years of linguistic research has proven beyond a shadow of a doubt that ASL is a language in its own right, separate from English. However, the majority of foreign language teachers know very little about ASL, and thus are very cautious when discussing it as a foreign language. Any progress would be slow, indeed, were we to take the route of change through the educational system.

Direct contact with a legislative member who works on educational issues made perfectly good sense to me. Thus, Assemblyman Jack O'Connell, Chairman of the Assembly Sub-Committee on Educational Reform, came to be the author of our California legislation.

Once AB 51 was introduced, an intense lobbying effort began. Now the time had come to connect with the foreign language teachers, parents organizations, various teachers organizations, and the State Department of Education. Many discussions were had and presentations delivered, utilizing statistics, linguistic information, and information regarding Deaf culture. I gathered proof of videotape libraries in existence, bibliographies of books, articles, films, and videotapes discussing ASL and Deaf culture, as well as materials which informed the public of Deaf cultural events such as "Celebration '87". I also solicited letters of support for the legislation from authorities in linguistics, educators, deaf organizations, and individuals from all walks of life.

As AB 51 moved through the legislative process, I continued to garner support, particularly in the form of letters and phone calls to members of the Senate and Assembly. I presented written and oral testimony before the Senate and Assembly, and requested professionals working with the Deaf community to provide expert testimony. In this way, no question was left unanswered, and concise, clear information was conveyed to the legislature.

When the bill had passed out of both houses of the legislative branch and reached the Governor's office, we had another battle on our hands. It underwent further scrutiny and, for some unknown reason, the Governor's analyst planned to advise him *not* to sign AB 51 into law. My heart sank, and I pooled all available resources in an attempt to change his mind. Once a bill reaches the Governor's office, no further testimony is heard; however, numerous phone calls, letters, and personal visits by our lobbying force were certainly allowed, and they paid off. The Governor signed AB 51 into law on July 24, 1987.

Over the course of ten months we brought an idea to fruition; through the rigorous legislative process, we created a law. Is this the end of the road? On the contrary, this is just the beginning of a challenging journey toward skillful teaching of ASL in high schools throughout the state.

An Academic Advisory Committee has been formed to work with the State Department of Education to implement this new law. Comprised of professionals in the field of education (six deaf, two hearing) and myself, the committee plans initially to address the following issues:

(1) **Curriculum**. My hope is that the state will adopt Vista College's model curriculum for use in the high schools. (Please refer to the article written about Vista's curriculum elsewhere in this journal.)

(2) **Teacher Credentialing**. How is an ASL teacher certified? What is the process? New tests need to be developed to suit ASL — a visual, gestural language.

(3) **Demand for ASL Classes**. We will locate current programs and encourage high schools to continue teaching ASL, keeping in mind the rigors of foreign language. We will also plan a campaign to inform the public about ASL and how AB 51 opens the door to learning this language.

(4) **Universities**. Although high school students may now satisfy graduation requirements for foreign language by taking courses in ASL, they will be unable to meet most universities' entrance requirements with this language. We plan to take this up with foreign language educators within the college and university systems to start a "grassroots" campaign to convince them that ASL does indeed meet the rigors of any foreign

language as a distinct, separate language apart from English. Throughout the country, colleges and universities have accepted ASL to meet their entrance requirements — on a challenge basis. We want to see this change so that ASL is accepted *always*.

Our committee met for the first time in early January of this year. Progress may be slow in materializing, but we *will* make a difference.

I have been contacted by numerous individuals throughout the country for "how to" information. Let me take a few minutes now to set forth the step-by-step process through which ASL legislation became reality in California.

(1) **Deaf Community**. Check the idea out with organizations and individuals. Understand how the community feels about such legislation. Garner support from the statewide association of the deaf and local agencies.

(2) **Research**. Do your research. Know where other ASL legislation exists. Know the statistics regarding deaf and hearing impaired populations in the country as well as your state. Be familiar with careers utilizing ASL, and know the location of videotape libraries within your state.

Make certain you understand that ASL is a separate and distinct language and are able to convey that clearly to others. Have materials in hand to support your statements.

Compile a list (including addresses and phone numbers) of professionals who will support your effort. These contacts will prove invaluable as you deal with teacher organizations, your state department of education, and so forth. These experts can give you needed information in succinct form as you prepare to lobby.

(3) **Choosing a Senator/Assemblyperson.** Take your idea to a legislative member knowledgeable in educational issues who has a prominent position with an education committee (preferably the chairperson). Be sure to research the various legislators prior to approaching any particular office; learn of their past voting record and the types of legislation he/she has authored in the past. You want a strong, successful person to carry this bill. Be sure you clarify this as an *educational* issue, not an issue about "the handicapped."

(4) **Legislative Consultants.** Now that you've found a senator/assemblyperson, meet the legislative aide/consultant who will handle your legislation. This is the person who will deal with the public entities and individuals who call to voice concern, support, or opposition. You need his/her utmost confidence in your skills, knowledge, and contacts so that as questions arise you will be contacted. You'll want to know of positive feedback that filters through the office, perhaps following up with a phone call or letter in some cases. It is also imperative that you be kept apprised of any negative rumblings so you can adequately prepare to lobby the person or entity who is questioning or opposing the legislation. The legislative aide is the key to a successful effort.

(5) **Lobbying.** Compile a list of your state's teachers organizations, educational organizations/associations, parents' organizations — any professional entity which deals with educational issues. Determine the name and phone number of the lobbyist for each, and through your legislative aide study their record in re-

gard to foreign language issues, particularly ASL. You may want to locate and hire a professional lobbyist depending on your expertise in this regard, as well as time constraints. You might contact lobbyists who deal with educational issues and ask for basic advice. I found these professionals most willing to discuss which approach best suited which organization, and I learned a great deal about what lay ahead in terms of opposition.

After the bill is introduced and you feel fully prepared, start contacting the lobbyists from the educational associations, and so forth. I presented a packet of supportive documentation to each person when I met. This packet included the statistics and supportive information that I mentioned earlier in the research section, along with letters of support from linguistic experts.

You also want to solicit letters of support from the deaf organizations in your state, linguistics experts around the country, educators, perhaps legislators in states where a similar law is in effect, and, of course, as many individuals as possible.

You will meet with opposition. This largely stems from basic misunderstanding of the language and culture of Deaf persons. Your job is to educate as you go along — most people will listen. They will ask who you are and what credentials you hold to speak intelligently of ASL. This is why all the backup documentation is so important. You, as an individual (or an agency), may not be "expert(s)" in linguistics, or "expert(s)" in the field of deafness, but there are those around the country who *are* experts, and who will gladly support you in your effort.

(6) **Testimony**. Be prepared to testify before the various legislative committees as the legislation is introduced. As the originator/sponsor, you must have at your fingertips information which will be required. Your senator/assemblyperson has a complex schedule and handles diverse legislation. You will be considered the expert — having answers to questions and concerns which will surface at hearings. I prepared written testimony, made enough copies for each member of the committee, and also prepared oral testimony. You may be asked to provide witnesses to support the legislation: locate educators, linguists to speak to the area of language, and deaf professionals to deal with the subject of culture. As you know, culture is part of any foreign language, and many people are skeptical when you propose that there is such a thing as Deaf culture. Be prepared to prove it.

(7) **Information Source**. This is you. You become a contact for people throughout your state who want more information on the legislation. Be prepared for this. Develop a circle of experts who are willing to discuss specific areas, i.e., Deaf culture, linguistics, ASL literature, and to whom you can refer calls. No one expects you to know it all. You must, however, be willing to research and come up with answers or referrals.

(8) **Sustained Effort**. Stick with it. Follow every step of the legislative process, making certain you're aware of any opposition which crops up. Contact, or ask your experts to contact, the potential opposition. Continue to solicit letters of support directed to members of the various senate and assembly committee members. You can't give up, but you do have time to breathe once in awhile.

(9) **Media**. The press is interested in this — it's different. In California, media coverage began when the bill was before the final Senate committee, continued through signature by the governor. Reporters are now interested in our implementation process. When you speak to the press, be clear, but do not hesitate to spread the word.

(10) **Follow-Up**. As in California, I suggest developing a committee to work with your state department of education toward effective implementation of your new law. I cannot stress enough the importance of this step in the process. Unless you continue on this path, your new law, can be set aside and prove meaningless. You've got to *make it happen*. Stay involved, and see to it that ASL is taught, not some coded form of English.

Remember to thank those who have worked with you, and those who have provided moral and/or financial support. These are very important people. Keep in mind that there are others out here working right along with you toward the same goals. Texas and Maine have adopted resolutions recognizing ASL as a foreign language, and in April 1987, Michigan officially mandated that ASL will meet their State's high school foreign language requirements. There is word from Ohio, Tennessee, and Illinois that ASL legislation is being considered. Keep a good, positive thought; this is important work!

Acceptance of American Sign Language at the University of New Mexico: The History of a Process

Lloyd Lamb and Phyllis Wilcox
University of New Mexico

The history of American Sign Language (ASL) in the United States is rich and varied. As other authors in this volume have demonstrated, ASL is a true natural language with its own culture and literary tradition. In spite of this rich and varied history, it is only within the past two or three decades that ASL has begun to gain recognition as a legitimate area of academic pursuit. With this recognition has come the realization that ASL might appropriately be seen as equivalent to a foreign language in fulfilling certain university graduation requirements.

Groups and individuals are now beginning to approach colleges and universities requesting the acceptance of ASL as a foreign language. Their requests often are met with resistance from administrators and faculty who claim that ASL is not a true language, lacks a culture, and possesses no body of literature.

ASL has been accepted in fulfillment of the undergraduate foreign language requirement at the University of New Mexico (UNM) since 1986. We are often asked, "At a time when many others were failing in similar efforts, what was the key to your success at UNM?" On the surface the decision was the culmination of a three-year effort initiated by one student, a major in the Bachelor of Science degree program in signed language interpreting. In reality, acceptance of ASL as a foreign language at UNM came about through a much longer period of planning, public relations, and hard work. This paper will briefly document the process which led to this acceptance.

The process began not in an effort to gain acceptance for ASL, but rather in our attempt to establish an interpreter training program at the baccalaureate level. Early in the 1970's, UNM began experiencing an increased interest in sign language similar to that being felt around the country. Beginning with a small group of eight students in a class offered by the Department of Communicative Disorders, the demand for sign language instruction soon was increasing at a much faster rate than we could reasonably meet. Not only were more students requesting existing courses, but there was a demand for more advanced courses in sign language. Slowly, a small program developed which offered beginning, intermediate, and advanced courses as well as a sign language practicum course. These courses were taught by one full-time lecturer and several part-time instructors. By 1978 the enrollment had grown to approximately 150 students each semester.

It soon became obvious that the need for well-trained, professional sign language interpreters in New Mexico had grown well beyond the supply. While students at UNM were getting good basic training in sign language studies, they were not sufficiently

prepared to meet the interpreting requirements specified in newly adopted federal and state regulations.

It was at this point that we first began discussing
the possibility of establishing a degree program in
signed language interpreting. After much consideration, we decided that a baccalaureate program would
be necessary to give students the knowledge and skills
they would need to effectively meet the broad demands of the interpreting profession.

Our experience within the university told us that in
attempting to establish a degree program, especially
one in a newly-emerging field that appeared to be
highly skilled oriented, we were likely to meet opposition. Further, we were aware of the rather cumbersome
bureaucracy through which any request of this nature
would have to move. For these and other reasons we
decided to adopt a cautious approach, to carefully
study the overall situation, and to plan for every fore-
seeable contingency. In retrospect, it is obvious that
this approach was crucial not only to the eventual acceptance of the degree program but also to acceptance
of ASL as a foreign language at UNM.

Our first step was to conduct a needs assessment focusing on the utilization of sign language interpreters
in New Mexico and throughout the United States. With
this, we were attempting to determine not only the
number of interpreters who might be needed in the future, but also specialty areas we might need to empha-
size in our program. Inquiries were made of the
National Association of the Deaf (NAD), the Registry
of Interpreters for the Deaf, the New Mexico Division
of Vocational Rehabilitation, independent living centers, the public schools, and several interpreter referral

centers in the Southwest. We began to contact interpreter training programs in an attempt to determine the numbers, types, and locations of other training programs around the country. Beginning with this early survey, we eventually found that there were eight (now only four) four-year programs and close to sixty newly established associate of arts programs in interpreting in the U.S. We were also able to estimate the number of trained interpreters available for work, to project future employment opportunities, and to compile sample curricula from numerous programs.

During the summer of 1979, we began contacting key individuals, agencies, and organizations within the state to inform them of our plans to initiate a program and to solicit input and support for the program. Among the agencies and organizations contacted were the New Mexico Association of the Deaf, the New Mexico Registry of Interpreters for the Deaf, the New Mexico Division of Vocational Rehabilitation, the Albuquerque Public Schools, the Social Security Administration, the Albuquerque Technical-Vocational Institute, and others.

In the fall of 1979, the first author, as chair of the Department of Communicative Disorders, contacted the university administration, for the first time introducing the idea of a four-year interpreter training program at UNM. At this point, we began soliciting letters of support from individuals around the state. Eventually, we received letters from parents of the deaf, speech-language pathologists, teachers and administrators in the public schools, teachers of satellite programs of the New Mexico School for the Deaf, practicing sign language interpreters, state legislators, deaf consumers, and others.

The first reaction of the university to our proposal was to suggest that we establish a two-year associate of arts in signed language interpreting. This recommendation was based on the belief that it would be easier to gain approval for a two-year program than a four-year bachelor level program. Almost a year was devoted to preparing a proposal for the two-year program. Included within the proposal were curriculum guides, course descriptions, needs assessment data, and supporting documentation.

It was at this point that we first learned just how lengthy and complicated a process we would have to follow in shepherding the proposal through all the required channels. We would expect it to travel through the Arts and Sciences Committee on Academic Programs and Curriculum, the Arts and Sciences faculty, the University Curriculum Committee, the Provost's Office, and finally to the Regents of the University. Eventually, the final proposal also faced the Undergraduate Academic Affairs Committee, the Senate Operations Committee, the UNM Faculty Senate, and the Library Committee. One or both of us attended every meeting, fielding countless questions from committee members and administrators.

In December 1980, after nearly two years of hard work and preparation, the Arts and Sciences Policy and Curriculum Committee voted to oppose an associate of arts degree, stating that it "violates the principles of educational breadth basic to a degree program in Arts and Sciences." The committee did, however, recommend that we submit a proposal for a four-year degree program, taking us back to the point where we had started two years earlier.

By this time, we had access to curricula from nearly sixty associate or bachelor level interpreter training programs. We expanded our initial proposal, taking into account the need to include the Arts and Sciences group requirements in mathematics, foreign languages, physical sciences, and so forth. The revised proposal once more began its arduous journey through the university bureaucracy. During this second go-around, we relied heavily upon the assistance of an Ad Hoc Advisory Committee which was established in the winter of 1981. The committee, which consisted of professors and chairs from several academic departments as well as representatives from the Albuquerque Public Schools, provided invaluable input for the proposal as well as political support. They also were able to help inform and educate their respective faculty, a fact that not only contributed to the ultimate approval of the degree program but also to the acceptance of ASL as a foreign language.

It cannot be emphasized enough how crucial a factor the administrators at the highest levels of the university were in providing support to our program. The fact that they read the related articles, books, and documentation connected with the situation and became aware of the actual merits of the argument meant smoother transition from the initital proposal to the final acceptance as an academic program. This would not have been possible without support from educated administrators, especially at the dean and associate provost levels.

The Bachelor of Science degree in Signed Language Interpreting was approved by the UNM Faculty Senate in December, 1982. Before the program was initiated the following fall, an Open Forum was held, sponsored jointly by the Department of Communicative Disorders and the New Mexico Association of the Deaf. Several nationally-known leaders in the deaf community participated, including Al Pimentel, Executive Directory of the NAD; Gary W. Olsen, Executive Director of the NAD Branch Office; and Herb Larson, an educator from California. Many deaf individuals from throughout New Mexico also attended the day-long forum. Through the forum, we were able to further inform interested parties of our plans, allay concerns expressed by members of the deaf community, and gain further support for the new program.

Finally, after several years of effort, the first interpreting majors began their studies in the fall of 1983. It was at this point that one of the first interpreting majors, Kim Corwin, petitioned the university to allow him to use ASL to meet the Arts and Sciences foreign language group requirement. This was not the first time such a request had been made. Previous requests, however, had been met with the response that ASL was not a language. Now that the College of Arts and Science had established a degree program, with courses specifically in ASL, a new objection was put forth: ASL may be a language, but it does not have a culture.

As with our efforts to establish the interpreting program, we again found that we were faced with the task of proving the validity of our request and fighting through a myriad of political obstacles. This time, however, we had history on our side. We again planned our approach very carefully. Following the lead that we had set in establishing our program, Mr. Corwin began collecting evidence in support of his proposal to accept ASL as a foreign language.

Many of the people who had been involved in establishing the interpreter training program were again willing to lend their support. Professors in linguistics spoke on behalf of the proposal. Administrators who just a few years previously had no background in the area were now aware of the linguistic and cultural facts and were eager to assist. Those administrators who were still skeptical were at least acquainted with the high academic quality of our program and thus were willing to listen to our case and to seek out information on their own. An assistant dean in the College of Arts and Sciences travelled to Northeastern University for a program on ASL research and came back convinced that the proposal had merit.

Like our effort to establish the interpreter training program, the proposal to accept ASL as a foreign language faced many obstacles. At one point, a sympathetic committee chairperson tabled the proposal in a committee meeting because he sensed that the members were leaning towards a negative vote. The following year, with different members, the proposal received a positive recommendation from this committee. Finally, in February 1986, the faculty of the College of Arts and Sciences voted unanimously to accept ASL in fulfillment of its foreign language requirements.

Our program is still evolving. Although ASL instruction and the interpreter training program, which now includes three full-time and five part-time faculty, began in the Department of Communicative Disorders, it became clear that this was not the most appropriate home for its future development. After a long process of negotiations (which had actually begun before the program was established), the faculty of the Department of Linguistics voted unanimously to invite the program and its faculty to join their department. This move has signalled the beginning of a new period of growth and development.

With the recent adoption of the Americans With Disabilities Act (ADA) has come an upsurge of awareness and commitment to citizens in the Deaf and Hard-of-Hearing communities throughout the nation. Our Department of Linguistics has done research into the need to expand and adapt the current program. There is extensive data available which indicates that our program should be changed into a baccalaureate degree in Signed Language Studies, where university students can study more extensively this bicultural, bilingual area. Students would have greater access to courses in American Deaf culture and ASL second language instruction, linguistics in ASL, Deaf history, language contact theories, ASL literature, fingerspelling theory and prediction strategies, and sociolinguistic and psycholinguistic aspects of deafness during their general liberal arts education. In addition, it is strongly believed that a master's degree in interpretation should be offered to allow interpreters to adequately prepare themselves for a lifetime of knowledge and dedication in the field of interpretation.

In conclusion, we would like to come back to the question with which we began this article. What was the key to our success in gaining acceptance of ASL as a foreign language at UNM? We believe that it rested in the fact that there has been a history of open discussion of and advocacy for ASL and Deaf culture at our university. The point is significant. In the pursuit of our goals, it is not enough to merely present compelling facts; it is also not enough to maintain high-quality, but isolated, programs. We must constantly seize the opportunity for advocacy and education, and we must encourage and participate in open dialogue among our students, colleagues, and community. It takes time, it is hard work, and at its worst it results in little more than frustration. At its best, however, it carries on the tradition of all that a university is meant to be.

Educating the American Sign Language Speaking Minority of the United States: A Paper prepared for the Commission on the Education of the Deaf

Harlan Lane
Northeastern University

The Commission on the Education of the Deaf has an historic opportunity to bring outmoded educational policy into line with recent scientific discoveries in linguistics and psychology, and thereby to right great wrongs in the education of a large percentage of America's deaf children.

Over the past decade there has been a rapid accumulation of evidence that the sign languages of the world are fully developed autonomous natural languages, with grammars and art forms all their own. Accordingly, the United Nations Educational Scientific and Cultural Organization has concluded that such languages should be "afforded the same status as other linguistic systems" and play "an active part in...educational programmes for the deaf."[1] American Sign Language has received particular study and informed scholars agree that ASL is one of our country's indigenous minority languages.[2] Several states have recently passed legislation providing for the teaching of ASL in their schools on the same basis as other indigenous and foreign minority languages in the United States.[3]

A second body of scientific investigation has demonstrated that a child who is unable to use language fluently at home and at school is severely disadvantaged in cognitive development and education.[4] The Congress of the United States has passed two types of statutes in recent years to remedy the disadvantage experienced by language-minority students who cannot communicate freely in the classroom by using their primary language: (a) The Bilingual Education Act (P.L. 89–10, Title VII, 1965 revised 1984, P.L. 98–511) provides funding for a wide variety of pro-

---

[1] *Consultation on the Different Approaches to Educating the Deaf.* Paris: UNESCO, 1985. (ed/84/ws/102)

[2] There is now a substantial literature: see for example H. Lane & F. Grosjean, *Recent Perspectives on ASL.* Hillsdale, NJ: Lawrence Erlbaum Asscociates 1980; R. Wilbur, *American Sign Language: Linguistic & Applied Dimensions.* San Diego: College Hill, 1987; J. Van Cleve (ed.) *Encyclopedia of Deaf People & Deafness.* NY: McGraw-Hill, 1986.

[3] E.g. California Assembly Bill 51. See also Selover, this volume.

[4] A. Willig, A Meta-analysis of selected studies on the effectiveness of bilingual education, *Review of Education Research* 55 (1985), 269–317. There is a substantial literature on the advantages accruing to deaf children from homes in which family members sign; see the review in M. Rodda and C. Grove, *Language, Cognition & Deafness.* Hillsdale, NJ: Lawrence Erlbaum Associates, 1987, pp. 304 ff. In a paper presented to the Tenth World Congress of the World Federation of the Deaf in July 1987, A. Weisel and J. Reichstein reported that Israeli deaf children of deaf parents had higher levels of reading comprehension, better emotional adjustment and self-image, and were more motivated to communicate with deaf and hearing people than their peers (matched on hearing loss and socioeconomic status) with hearing parents.

grams promoting the use of minority languages in the schools; and (b) civil rights statutes (P.L. 88–352, Title VI, 1964, and P.L. 93–380, 1974) impose an affirmative duty on the schools to afford children who speak a minority language an equal educational opportunity by lowering the English-language barrier.

Thus, there exists legislation to protect language minorities; there is also legislation to protect the handicapped; but those children who become members of a language minority because of their handicap are not protected: they have fallen into the crack between two bureaucracies. Lacking the recent evidence that ASL is a minority language, the Federal agencies entrusted with promoting the education and the rights of minority language users have heretofore dismissed deaf ASL users as merely handicapped, while agencies charged with ensuring effective education for the handicapped have, understandably, dismissed the central educational issue for many deaf children — their minority-language status — and have attempted to serve them as all other classes of handicapped children, whose education is already conducted in their primary language.

It has been shown repeatedly that children whose primary language is ASL, like those who speak other minority languages such as Spanish or Navaho, are at a severe educational disadvantage in a system that disbars, denigrates, and denies their primary language.[5] It is reasonable to believe that the same educational remedies provided by the Congress and the courts for the speakers of all other minority languages will benefit ASL-speaking children. In any case, it is the law. Recognizing that ASL is one of the minority languages of the United States, the Commission on the Education of the Deaf can close the bureaucratic gap by urging that the competent Federal agencies apply existing statutes and regulations, by requesting that the Congress appropriate funds for this purpose, and by incorporating this recognition in its pertinent recommendations.

1. **The Bilingual Education Act**. The motivating policy and the definitions of the Bilingual Education Act, as well as the regulations issued by the Department of Education to implement the act, all suggest the appropriateness of grant applications that address the educational needs of children whose primary language is ASL. Indeed, such children are particularly disadvantaged by an English-only education. Like their Spanish-speaking counterparts, they are receiving their education in a language they are struggling to learn. Unlike them, however, most have no familiarity with any other spoken language and cannot hear English, which they must learn by indirect means. In setting forth its motivation, the Act states:

> (1) that there are large and growing numbers of children of limited English proficiency; (2) that many of such children have a cultural heritage which differs from that of English proficient per-

---

[5] Large population, national surveys have shown that the average deaf high school student has the academic achievement of hearing students half his or her age. A comparison of 1974 and 1983 academic achievement scores of hearing-impaired students shows that this disadvantage has not changed during the past decade, in which most schools have subscribed to **English-based** manual sign communication, called *Total Communication*. A. Schildroth and M. Karchmer, *Deaf Children in America*. San Diego: College Hill, 1986.

sons; (3) that the Federal Government has a special and continuing obligation to assist in providing equal educational opportunity to limited English proficient children; (4) that the Federal Government has a special and continuing obligation to assist language-minority students to acquire the English language proficiency that will enable them to become full and productive members of society; (5) that a primary means by which a child learns is through the use of such child's native language and cultural heritage; (6) that therefore large numbers of children of limited English proficiency have educational needs which can be met by the use of bilingual educational methods and techniques; ...(20 USCS 3222).

The Code of Federal Regulations delineates the limited-English-proficiency students to whom the act applies. The wording makes clear that children whose primary language is ASL, whether or not they learned it from their parents, are directly affected. Included are

[individuals] whose native language is other than English ... 'Native language,' when used with reference to an individual of limited English proficiency, means the language normally used by the individual. If the language normally used by the child cannot be determined, the language normally used by the parents or legal guardians of the child is the child's native language. (500.4; 34 CFR Ch. V, 7/1/87 edition)

All of the following programs are currently funded by the Bilingual Education Act to benefit limited-English-proficiency children in various language minorities, and many of these programs could have a significant impact on the educational achievement of ASL-speaking children:

Basic Programs
Academic Excellence Programs
Family English Literacy Programs
Special Populations Programs
State Educational Agency Programs
Evaluation Assistance Center Programs
Educational Personnel Training Programs
Fellowships Programs
Training Development and Improvement Programs
Short-Term Training Programs
Multifunctional Resource Center Programs

Bilingual-bicultural instruction includes: academic "subject matters" taught, transitionally at least, in the pupil's primary language; English as a Second Language (ESL); the history, culture, and language arts of the student's minority-language group; American culture and history. The goal is to teach the student English so that he or she can ultimately be educated exclusively in English, while assuring that the student does not fall behind in other studies. This objective is met by fostering a healthy self-image, by the development of cognitive powers, by creating a bridge to the child's existing linguistic and cultural knowledge, and by developing reading and expressive skills in English.

The potential advantages of extending such bilingual-bicultural programs to ASL-using children are similar to those for other language-minority children. There would be an infusion of new ideas and methods for teaching this minority, including new strategies for teaching them English, improved English literacy, improved academic achievement scores, improved emotional adjustment, decreased need for counseling services, increased class size without reduction in individualized attention, decreased dropout rates, decreased underemployment on leaving school, increase in bilingual fluency of classroom teachers, teaching careers opened to adult minority-language users, enhanced teacher-pupil communication, and enhanced parental communication with teachers and pupils. Among the potential disadvantages are the reduction in the time available to use English when some classes are taught in ASL, and the increased burden on monolingual teachers to develop bilingual capability.[6]

Proposed Recommendation 1

The Secretary of Education should take affirmative action to encourage applications under the Bilingual Education Act that seek to enhance the quality of education received by limited-English-proficiency children whose native (primary) language is American Sign Language.

2. **Civil rights legislation.** In an historic ruling that greatly promoted bilingual education in the United States, the Supreme Court ruled in Lau v. Nichols, that Title VI of the Civil Rights Act of 1964 requires local school authorities receiving Federal financial assis-

---

[6] J. D. Haft, Assuring equal educational opportunity for language-minority students; Bilingual education and the Equal Educational Opportunity Act of 1974, *Columbia Journal of Law & Social Problems* 18 (1983), 209–293.

tance to provide special instruction to language-minority students:

> Basic English skills are at the very core of what...-
> public schools teach. Imposition of a requirement
> that, before a child can effectively participate in
> the educational program, he must already have
> acquired those basic skills, is to make a mockery
> of public education. We know that those who do
> not understand English are certain to find their
> classroom experience wholly incomprehensible
> and in no way meaningful. (414 UA at 566)

The 1974 Equal Education Opportunity Act requires local authorities to take "appropriate action to overcome language barriers that impede equal participation in the instructional program" (20 USC sec 1703f,1976). Speaking in behalf of this legislation, President Nixon said: "This Act would further establish an educational bill of rights for Mexican Americans, Puerto Ricans, Indians and others who start their education under language handicaps to make certain that they, too, will have equal opportunity" (118 Cong Rec 8928, 1972). In Rios v. Read, the Court ruled that the two statutes cited and others "mandate teaching such children subject matter in their native tongue (when required) by competent teachers...and [strongly suggests the requirement of a] bicultural [component] as a psychological support to the subject matter instruction" (480 F Supp at 22). The Court found that the school district was not in compliance merely by providing students with intensive training in English (while they fell behind in their other subjects, which required a knowledge of English); the Court ordered school officials to add three features to their bilingual education program: to educate teachers about the special cultural problems of minority language children, to train all instructors in the teaching of English as a foreign language, and actively to seek and employ instructors of the same ethnic group as the minority students.

In other cases the Supreme Court ruled that language barriers addressed by the Equal Education Opportunity Act need not involve a foreign language but may involve an indigenous American language (Guadalupe v. Tempe Elementary School District), or an English dialect departing significantly from standard American English (Martin Luther King Elementary School Children v. Michigan Board of Education). Thus it seems reasonable to believe that the protection of language minorities provided by these statutes, and others cited in these and related cases, should and does extend to children who belong to the ASL-speaking minority. These children are thus discriminated against in monolingual English schools, and the remedy is a bilingual-bicultural program. To be in compliance with the law of the land, such a program would likely have the following phases:

1. a pre-program phase of assistance to minority-language preschoolers;
2. an identification process for placement of ASL-speaking children in appropriate programs;
3. instruction provided, at least transitionally, using the minority language;
4. instruction in English using special bilingual materials;
5. tests for periodically assessing abilities, to admit students who need the program and to exit

those who have attained sufficient English fluency; and

6. program evaluation.

Proposed Recommendation 2

The Commission on the Education of the Deaf finds that current educational programs are frequently inequitable with regard to children whose primary language is American Sign Language, and frequently limit the full participation of such individuals in our society. It enjoins the Office of Civil Rights of the Department of Education to identify all educational programs with more than twenty children whose primary language is American Sign Language and which do not provide bilingual-bicultural programs, to notify such programs of their noncompliance with Federal laws and regulations, and to seek sanctions as appropriate for continued noncompliance.

3. **Taking account of ASL-speaking children in other recommendations of the Commission.**

Appropriate Education, Recommendation 3

(Proposed addition to part (f) of draft recommendation 1 concerning the Individualized Educational Plan):

In order to respect the linguistic needs of the child, those children whose primary language is American Sign Language should receive a bilingual-bicultural education wherever possible, as provided under the Bilingual Education Act of 1965.

Personnel training, Recommendation 4

Appropriate educational placement of deaf children, including bilingual-bicultural education of children whose primary language is American Sign language, requires specialists to evaluate the linguistic competencies of deaf children. These specialists must themselves be competent in English and ASL, as well as knowledgeable about: the linguistic structure and use of both languages; the language arts and cultural contexts of communication in both languages; the principles of linguistics and psychometrics as they affect the design, use, and interpretation of language tests; English-based methods of manual communication such as Total Communication, Signed English, Cued speech, etc.; and other subjects. The Secretary of Education should solicit proposals for the creation of model training programs to supply such bilingual language-evaluation specialists.

Personnel training, Recommendation 5

Because ASL is the primary language of large numbers of deaf children, because many of these children will increasingly be educated in bilingual-bicultural programs as awareness of their minority-language status grows, and because the preponderance of deaf children are members of the ASL-using community in adulthood, teachers of the deaf increasingly require at least basic fluency in ASL, an awareness of ASL structure and use, and a knowledge of the history and culture of this language minority. The Secretary of Education should contract for a reexamination of teacher-training programs and criteria for their Federal

funding with a view to fostering greater bilingual-bicultural competencies among special educators of the
deaf.

Personnel training, Recommendation 6

Because successful education of language-minority
children requires the enhancement of self-image and
the presence of role models, every effort should be
made to involve ASL-fluent adults in the education of
ASL speaking children, including such roles as teachers, counselors, media and library workers, residence
advisors, communication aides or specialists, pre-
school recreation coordinators, etc.

Umbrella recommendation 7

Because the Commission on the Education of the Deaf
recognizes that deaf children whose primary language
is American Sign Language are members of an indigenous language minority and comprise a large proportion of all those children whose education it seeks to
enhance, the Commission desires that all of its recommendations for legislation by the Congress and for implementation by the Secretary of Education be
followed with sensitivity to the extensive bilingual-bicultural needs and skills of many of America's deaf
children. Initiatives in model programs, materials development, teacher training, educational technology,
basic research, and so forth should always be under-
taken with a view to utilizing for educational goals the
substantial fluency in ASL language, language arts,
and culture possessed by numerous deaf school children.

Some Notes on ASL as a "Foreign" Language

David F. Armstrong
Gallaudet University

Introduction

Those who would promote ASL as a "foreign" language for purposes of higher education instruction and the satisfaction of curriculum requirements must take account of the several ways in which it is foreign to the hearing people who will be asked to make decisions about its status. Several ways in which ASL is foreign are listed here, in order of increasing strangeness. First, it is foreign in the same way as spoken languages with which the hearing person is unfamiliar — namely, as an unknown tongue. Second, it is even more foreign in that it employs a communication channel separate from that used by spoken languages; and, thus, has structural characteristics that distinguish it from spoken languages. Third, it is employed by a subgroup within the larger American society that is not, on the surface, otherwise distinguishable from the latter — in fact, it is used as a first language by the deaf children of hearing people who are unfamiliar with it. All of these factors combine to make ASL, from the point of view of most hearing Americans, a language of surpassing strangeness, indeed. It seems self-evident that these factors have combined to make the decision to accept

or not to accept ASL as a foreign language a difficult
one for many university administrators, but I will argue as well that ramifications of these factors combine
to make the same decision problematic from the point
of view of the deaf community as well.

General Observations on the Status of ASL as a Language of Instruction in American Higher Education

Most readers of this book will not need an introduction
to the arguments that have been adduced in support of
and in opposition to the proposition that ASL is a well
formed human language, and I will not reiterate them
here. It remains the case however, that there are well
educated people who occupy positions of authority in
American universities who do not accept the idea that
ASL is a legitimate human language (although Corwin
and Wilcox (1985) suggest that the number may be
small). It is to be hoped that further work such as that
begun by Wilcox and others will have the effect of reducing the extent if not the depth of the ignorance.

The primary argument that is advanced against the
worthiness of ASL to be accepted into the higher education curriculum has to do with the third "strangeness" factor cited above — namely, that the language is
used only by a subculture, that it has not developed as
a scholarly language and as a consequence possesses
no literature. This a serious charge that is open to only
partial refutation. Corwin and Wilcox (1985) have recently summarized the scholarly literature concerning
the extensive oral literature of the deaf community in
ASL and have thereby strengthened the rationale for
allowing ASL to fulfill second language requirements
in higher education. Moreover, aspects of literary the-

ory are being brought to bear on ASL literature, especially in the area of poetics (Cohn, 1986). Strong arguments for the existence of a deaf culture are presented by Rutherford in this book; and in his chapter, Chapin argues the case for accepting ASL as a "foreign" language along the lines just presented, as does Wilbers. It remains the case, however, that ASL has not been developed as a scholarly language in its own right and for that reason does not currently possess the power, as an intellectual tool, of English and other world languages that have highly developed written literatures in the arts and sciences. Whether it will be so developed remains to be seen. However, Hymes (1973: 78) has pointed out that it would be difficult for any language other than the small number that have achieved this status to be so developed.

This final point generally proves to be the most difficult obstacle for those promoting ASL as an alternative second language in higher education, but the arguments developed by Wilcox, Chapin and others should be powerful enough to overcome it. A fundamental question for deaf people, however, concerns the circumstances under which ASL should be considered an appropriate *first* language for university students. A large majority of the deaf students at Gallaudet University consider themselves to be bilingual in English and ASL (Kannapell, 1985), and it is probably safe to assume that this would not be atypical of deaf students elsewhere. Within a population of deaf students, one assumes that a large percentage who consider themselves bilingual would also consider ASL to be their first language. In American higher education institutions, the ordinary expectation is that students at the bachelor's level should acquire a working or functional knowledge of a second language other than their own and should achieve mastery of their first language. By mastery is meant the ability to enter fluently into the most highly developed artistic and rhetorical uses of the language, at least by way of appreciation if not creation.

For deaf students, then, English may be the "foreign" language, and at least one deaf student has successfully argued this case at a major U.S. university (Wilbers, 1987). We could envision a more general bachelor's level curriculum that would allow deaf students to designate either ASL or English as a first language and the other as a second or "foreign" language. For assessment purposes, the student would be required to demonstrate mastery only in the first language and some specified level of functional skill in the other. As virtually all American universities are English language institutions, one would imagine that assessment criteria in English as a second language would include a functional level sufficient for effective performance in subject area courses taught in English.

General acceptance of a curricular proposal such as this would have the salutary effect of putting the assessment shoe on the right linguistic foot. It is unfair to expect all deaf students to perform at a mastery level in English when they have had to learn it through a process similar to that employed in teaching classical languages to hearing students. Lane (1984: 334) has said it best:

> Hartford pupils [that is, students at the American School for the Deaf in the mid 19th Century]... can write English as well as any Yale student can

write Latin. Moreover, that is sufficient. Our society does not require people whose native language is not English to write English flawlessly
— only understandably.

This is not to suggest that deaf students cannot
achieve mastery of English or that they should not be
encouraged to attempt to do so. Obviously many prelingually deaf students can and do achieve mastery of
English, and they should demand environments in
which their potential to do so is maximized, but they
should not be held accountable if they cannot. For purposes of qualifying for a baccalaureate degree they
should be held accountable for qualifying at a mastery
level in either ASL or English. By the same token, the
educational system should be held accountable for en-
abling deaf students to use effectively whatever English functional level they do achieve.

The question whether ASL should be accepted in
fulfillment of second language requirements for hearing students is, it seems to me, more problematic, especially from the point of view of deaf people themselves,
and that question will be explored in greater depth below.

The Function of ASL in Boundary Maintenance

Most deaf people have viewed the opening up of ASL
to linguistic study as a positive development in the
growth of their community's self-esteem and public
image. For example, the National Association of the
Deaf awarded the founder of scientific ASL research a
festschrift at its 1980 meeting (Baker and Battison,
1980). However, deaf people may want to be concerned about the spread of knowledge about and ex-

pertise in ASL for two principal reasons. First, there is the question of what effect scientific study itself may have upon the language. Second, there is the question of the potential effect on the deaf community of a large number of hearing ASL users.

I addressed the first of these questions, at least obliquely, in an article published in 1984. In that article, I urged the (mostly hearing) people who study ASL to describe the language in its own iconic terms and not to force the language "onto the procrustean bed of structural linguistics (Armstrong, 1984:179-180)." This comment was interpreted by McCay Vernon (1987:159, 163) in a way that I had not anticipated but in a way that has great relevance here. Vernon assumed that I was critiquing the ways in which the structure of English has been imposed on sign language for the creation of surrogate educational systems such as Signed English. Vernon is quite right in making his point, but what I had in mind is the damage that may be done to ASL itself when an analytic system devised for the description of spoken languages is imposed on a language in the visual medium. Should we expect that as these analytic strategies are imposed and results from them published that there will be a long term effect on the evolution of the language itself? And if that should prove to be the case, would it be good, bad or neutral? I believe that these are questions that deaf people might want to ask themselves as they consider the potential benefits of increased scrutiny of their language and culture by hearing people.

Mindess (1990: 9–10) has recently presented evidence that linguistic analysis may already be having an effect on the signing of deaf people. It is especially important to note here that the work being cited by the deaf signers was itself conducted by a deaf linguist:

> The three respondents who had either read Supalla's (unpublished) paper or heard about it, cited his work on arbitrary name signs as the definitive description. One man said that before he had heard of Supalla's work he had thought that anything was acceptable, but now he knows better and has changed his name sign.[1]

I take an agnostic position with respect to whether or not this is beneficial, especially because all of the people involved are deaf. However, it is important to recognize that conscious management of the evolution of the language (other than by those interested in making it more English-like) may have begun, and it is important that deaf people consider its possible implications

Returning to Vernon's original point, cited above, I also take an agnostic position. There is no a priori reason for assuming that evolution of ASL that brought it structurally closer to English would necessarily be bad either — it might even be good. However, the situation calls for planning and management of the evolution, and this planning should involve deaf people.

The second question that I posed reflects the phrase in the title of this section — the function of ASL in boundary maintenance. I follow Hymes (1971: vii) in suggesting that a major function of surface complexity in language is impenetrability — that is, that languages are complex and difficult to learn partly for adaptive reasons, so that in-group and out-group members may easily be identified by native speakers. Skill in ASL

---

[1] The work referred to is now published as Supalla 1990 (Ed.)

serves the same function for deaf people. This may be one reason why deaf people (despite some resentment) have tended to accept surrogate forms of signing, such as PSE, in their communication with hearing people. From this perspective, PSE could be seen as a buffer between the deaf community and hearing signers (Markowicz and Woodward, 1982). If large numbers of hearing people were to begin learning ASL, at what point would they become a threat to the integrity of the deaf community? What critical mass of hearing ASL signers would be needed to make them the dominant force in the evolution of the language? How would deaf people respond to such a development? A partial answer to the latter question can be found in the history of black English — an in-group responds to a cultural invasion of outsiders by staying one step ahead of them through the constant creation of new forms (in this regard see Wilcox (1984) for a telling example of semantic shift in a standard ASL sign designed by deaf students to befuddle their teachers).

This point is not trivial. Before we begin to advocate too strongly the widespread acceptance of ASL as a "foreign" language for curricular purposes, and the consequent large increase in the number of hearing signers (see Nash 1987), perhaps we should learn if deaf people would really welcome a vastly increased signing community. It appears self-evident that deaf people would benefit from having more hearing people who could communicate with them, but it seems equally likely that at some point defensive mechanisms for boundary maintenance would start to appear. There is some direct evidence that deaf people are becoming uncomfortable about the recent growth in numbers of hearing signers: "Some [deaf] people expressed the feeling that 'hearing people are taking over more now'" (Mindess, 1990: 14).

Conclusion

I would like to end with a plea for a more radical science of ASL and the deaf community that would be based on much greater involvement by deaf people themselves in the study of their language and culture. In entering this plea I am not ignorant of the fact that the lives of deaf and hearing people are inextricably intertwined, and I am convinced that hearing people have a legitimate interest in the deaf community. I am also cognizant of the fact that the hearing people who have studied ASL have been uncommonly responsible and responsive to the needs and desires of the deaf community. What I am suggesting is that we join with Hymes (1973: 81) in calling for safeguards to ensure that the anthropology of the deaf community is, in his terms, "mediative" and does not become a tool for manipulation:

> Anthropology, for instance, is fairly described as the study of colored people by whites [or of deaf people by hearing people]. That matrix has changed irreversibly. A science of man limited to certain societies or interests was always implicitly a contradiction in terms; increasingly, it has become an impossibility or a monstrosity. Knowledge about people is a resource, like control of oil and of armies.... Thus universalization of the science of man must mean extension not only to all countries of participation, but to all communities. The proper role of the scientist, and the goal of his efforts, should not be "extractive,"

> but mediative. It should be to help communities
> be ethnographers of their own situations, to re-
> late their knowledge usefully to general knowl-
> edge, not merely to test and document. Such a
> role could be the safeguard of both the intellectu-
> al and the ethical purposes of the science itself.

How could such increased involvement by deaf people be accomplished? There are two principal needs that have to be addressed: training and employment opportunities. I believe that these needs are interrelated. First, the institutions doing the ethnography and linguistics need to make public commitments regarding levels of employment within their departments for members of the ethnic or minority group (in this case the deaf community) being studied. Second, these departments must make commitments to provide the necessary monetary support for those to be trained to occupy the positions. But the public commitment regarding employment levels is the key. White Anglo-Saxon Able-bodied Males in our society can afford the luxury of training for possibly non-existent careers in fields such as anthropology and nevertheless expect to find gainful professional employment in fields only marginally related to the field of training (the current author is a case in point). Members of minority groups have usually felt that they could not afford this luxury and have tended to opt for training in professional fields such as law, medicine, teaching or engineering that appeared to afford employment prospects. The only way to attract substantial numbers of deaf people to fields such as anthropology and linguistics is through the publication of credible affirmative action goals for employment by the institutions doing the research. And in the final analysis, the only way to take the "foreignness" out of ASL is to bring deaf people in larger numbers into U.S. universities as full-fledged members of the academic community.

References

Armstrong, D. 1984. "Scientific and Ethical Issues in the Case for American Sign Language," *Sign Language Studies*, 43, 165-184.

Baker, C. & R. Battison. 1980 *Sign Language and the Deaf Community: Essays in Honor of William C. Stokoe*, Silver Spring, Md.: National Association of the Deaf.

Cohn, J. 1986 "The New Deaf Poetics: Visible Poetry," *Sign Language Studies*, 52, 263-277.

Corwin, K. & S. Wilcox. 1985 "The Search for the Empty Cup Continues," *Sign Language Studies*, 48, 249-268.

Hymes, D. 1971"Foreword," in *The Origin and Diversification of Language*, by Morris Swadesh, Chicago: Aldine.

Hymes, D. 1973 "On the Origins and Foundations of Inequality among Speakers," *Dædalus*, Summer, 59-86.

Kannapell, B. 1985 "Language Choice Reflects Identity Choice: A Sociolinguistic Study of Deaf College Students," Doctoral Dissertation, Georgetown University, Washington, D.C.

Lane, H. 1984 *When the Mind Hears*, N. Y.: Random House.

Markowicz, H. and J. Woodward. 1982. "Language and the maintenance of ethnic boundaries in the deaf community." In J. Woodward, *How You Gonna Get to Heaven If You Can't Talk With Jesus?* Silver Spring, MD: TJ Publishers.

Mindess, A. 1990. "What name signs can tell us about deaf culture." *Sign Language Studies,* 66, 1–24.

Nash, J. 1987 "Policy and Practice in the American Sign Language Community," *Int. J. Soc. Lang.,* 68, 7-22.

Supalla, S. 1990. "The arbitrary name sign system in American Sign Language." *Sign Language Studies,* 67, 99–126.

Vernon, M. 1987 "Controversy within Sign Language," *The ACEHI Journal,* 12, 3, 155-164.

Wilbers, S. 1987 "Learning to Accept Sign Language as Natural, Complete," Minneapolis *Star and Tribune,* April 12, 35A.

Wilcox, S. 1984 "STUCK in School: A Study of Semantics in a Deaf Education Class," *Sign Language Studies,* 43, 141-164.